Seven by Seven

Seven Virtues to
Teach Your Child
by Age Seven

L. Roo McKenzie, Ed.D.

WESTBOW
PRESS®
A DIVISION OF THOMAS NELSON
& ZONDERVAN

Scriptures taken from the Holy Bible, New International Version®, NIV®. Copyright © 1973, 1978, 1984, 2011 by Biblica, Inc.™ Used by permission of Zondervan. All rights reserved worldwide. www.zondervan.com The "NIV" and "New International Version" are trademarks registered in the United States Patent and Trademark Office by Biblica, Inc.™

WestBow Press books may be ordered through booksellers or by contacting:

WestBow Press
A Division of Thomas Nelson & Zondervan
1663 Liberty Drive
Bloomington, IN 47403
www.westbowpress.com
1 (866) 928-1240

Because of the dynamic nature of the Internet, any web addresses or links contained in this book may have changed since publication and may no longer be valid. The views expressed in this work are solely those of the author and do not necessarily reflect the views of the publisher, and the publisher hereby disclaims any responsibility for them.

Any people depicted in stock imagery provided by Thinkstock are models, and such images are being used for illustrative purposes only. Certain stock imagery © Thinkstock.

ISBN: 978-1-5127-9819-7 (sc)
ISBN: 978-1-5127-9820-3 (hc)
ISBN: 978-1-5127-9818-0 (e)

Library of Congress Control Number: 2017912056

Print information available on the last page.

WestBow Press rev. date: 12/19/2017

Dedication

Lovingly dedicated to my first grandchild,
Olivia Grace McKinney.

May you and every child, benefit from the pages
of this book, and may you grow in grace,
and in the knowledge of Jesus Christ,
the loving Father and eternal friend of little children.

Contents

Acknowledgements

Serendipity may bring unexpected blessings sometimes, but intentionality is generally more reliable. The inspiration to write this book did not happen by serendipity. The birth of my first grandchild, Olivia Grace, stimulated the desire to create a tangible product from ideas that I had long been pre-occupied with from my days as a high school principal in California. The obvious struggles of parents and teachers, and the desire for a better world for my grandchild provided the impetus to get this work done. I thank her and the many passionate individuals who contributed their talents and insights to the process of bringing this work to fruition.

I am particularly grateful to Dr. Grace Virtue for technical help and editorial guidance, and to Dr. Audley Dwyer, my principal and English teacher at Harrison Memorial High School, for editorial help. Thanks as well to countless friends who encouraged me to write this book, and scores of others who shared with me the importance of these virtues to them and their children.

Finally, thanks to my parents Terrence and Muriel McKenzie, for consistently modeling the seven virtues explained in the chapters that follow, and for being my first inspiration to write this book. Thanks to my daughters, Maritza and Kari-Ann, who uphold the family's traditions by striving to live these virtues, and again to Olivia Grace, who provided the final burst of inspiration to get this work done.

L. Roo McKenzie, Ed.D.

Introduction

The Children are Watching

"For I have chosen him, so that he will direct his household after him, to keep the way of the Lord to do what is right and just."

(Genesis 18:19)

Children are the heartbeat of God. Just as He gave Adam and Eve the breath of life at their creation, so also does He breathe life into every boy and girl fashioned in the wombs of their mothers. Ours is the special privilege as parents to treat them with tenderness, respect, and love and to guide them into making intelligent choices based upon the eternal principles of God's character and kingdom.

It is undeniable that spiritually speaking, all children are born with a defect. It is called sin. This defect leaves every child with an almost irresistible proclivity to practice vices rather than virtues. It is not only a sacred responsibility, but also a divine honor to be a parent who can help to counteract the effects of this deadly malady and prepare their children for eternity. Indeed, parenting must begin with eternity in mind, for children are given to us to help populate the kingdom of heaven. Gospel-powered and purpose-driven parenting begins before conception and lasts beyond the days of childhood. The effects of parenting last for an eternity—eternal life *with* God or eternal separation *from* God.

Parenting is definitely one of the happiest and most rewarding undertakings of our lives, but it is also a most daunting responsibility. Fortunately for those of us dedicated to Godly parenting, we have the word of God; He is not in the business of giving advice or suggestions, for He knows what is *right* and *best* for our children and His instructions are explicit in the Scriptures.

God, the all-knowing Father of all children declares, "These commandments that I give you today are to be upon your hearts. Impress them upon your children. Talk about them when you sit at home and when you walk along the road, when you lie down and when you get up." (Deuteronomy 6:6-7)

The home is not only the first school of children, but also the first and most important school of virtues where they begin to develop a biblical worldview that clarifies the role of God in their character development. If parents, who are God's agents on earth, neglect Him and their children, it is almost certain that their children will neglect God and their parents also. Children's conception of who God is, is largely dependent upon who their parents are and what they do. Hence, the early education of children initiated through the God-given responsibility of parenting should not be out-sourced to other individuals or institutions. "No educational system, no matter how well designed and executed, can make up for that which is not given to children in their homes."[1]

President Theodore Roosevelt, in 1908, at the First International Congress on the Child, expressed the same idea with even deeper intensity when he wrote: "There are exceptional women, there are exceptional men, who have other tasks to perform in addition to the task of motherhood and fatherhood ... but it is the task that is connected with the home that are the fundamental tasks of humanity."[2]

The home is the place where love and the virtues of Christ speak and act, and God will call for an accounting of His heritage, just like the merchant in the parable of the loaned money did on his return from his long journey (Matthew 25:14-30). Parents will not be able to enter a "guilty-with-explanation-plea," like the servant who had received the one talent attempted to do. Children are on loan to us as parents, and the day will surely come when their Father will enquire of us, "Where is the flock that was entrusted to you ...?" (Jeremiah 13:20).What will the answer be? If parents, because of their own lack of discipline, set their children on a wrong trajectory in reverence, obedience, order, meditation, surrender, generosity and trust, will God not hold them accountable?

The greatest gift of God to the world was wrapped up in a child—Mary's tiny little baby, Emanuel, God with us. Children are God's next greatest gift to humanity and heaven's best commercial. When Jesus desired to show men what His Father's kingdom looked like, He called unto Himself a little child and said, "I tell you the truth, unless you change and become like little children, you will never enter the kingdom of heaven" (Matthew 18:3). Children *are* heaven's best commercial.

The values and virtues of the character and kingdom of God are in direct opposition to the values and vices of the character and kingdom of Satan. The "village"–secular society–has assertively taken over the job of informing and educating our children about the values in which it believes. It has become increasingly clear in our postmodern world, that these are *not* values that are congruent with the character of God or the values of His kingdom. It is an urgent and God-honoring imperative that parents assertively take back from society (the media, the entertainment industry, the secularists, and the anti-God forces) the job of training their children in the values and virtues of God.

World Views

A worldview is the eye of the mind, soul, and body, and is subliminally influenced by what we see, hear, experience, value, and do. There are only two worldviews that really matter—the biblical and the secular. At the heart of either worldview is a belief about who God is. From the time of their birth, children begin to develop their worldview through which they see and interpret God, the universe and the forces of good and evil. Having a worldview is not optional, for a child's mind will not be left blank. If it is not informed by the forces of good (God), it will be informed by the forces of evil (Satan). Neutrality is not an option. Never has and never will. Worldviews are subversive forces—one will always strive to subvert the other until the day Jesus returns.

Parents as Programmers

The whole world is enjoying the benefits of computer technology. Computers not only have to be built, but they also have to be programmed to perform specific functions. Our children come to us made by God but infected by the sin virus, inherited from their fore-parents, Adam and Eve. They are pre-programmed to sin and rebel against God. Parents are God's earthly programmers who are tasked with the responsibility of cooperating with the Holy Spirit to re-program the minds and hearts of their children to develop the virtues and graces that will help them experience the restoration of the image of God in them. God holds the rights to our children because He made them, and parents have the responsibility of raising them as godly offspring because they birthed them.

Parents are also cultivators and triggers. They cultivate in the character of their children the seeds of the virtues of Christ, and also trigger in them the start of a life of transformation and restoration into the image of their Maker. The virtues of Christ are not psychological theories that have been developed by virtue-deprived and spiritually-depraved theorists. Instead, they are attributes of the character of God that are transferable to the character of His children. The seven virtues presented in this book must speak first to the heart and mind before they speak to the sensory organs. These seven virtues are not so much behaviors to display as they are graces to imbibe and embrace. For the values and virtues of Christ are not like beads on a string that can be worn as ornaments. They are inner, spirit-based, transforming graces that do their best work from the inside out. These virtues are rated "PG," for indeed, parents must begin giving guidance to their development from the first year of a child's life. Virtues are like health; they are necessary for balanced living. Like health, they are not tangible or visible, but when they are absent from the life the effects are immediately observable. Living the virtues of Christ is divine grace in motion in humanity.

Under Construction

Young children are under construction. The concrete of their tender minds and characters is still wet. They are impressionable and easily influenced by what they are exposed to. Many scholars agree that that the worldview and values of children are 95 percent established by age 11. It is incumbent, therefore, upon God-honoring parents to take the initiative and model, teach, and instill in their children a biblical worldview that will influence the development of their virtues and help them to "grow in the grace and in the knowledge of our Lord and Savior Jesus Christ" (2 Peter 3:18).

The choices parents are making *today* for their children are the choices that will make their children *tomorrow*. Moral education—the training of the heart and mind toward good—is first and foremost the work of parents. It was William Bennett who once wrote: "Moral education must provide training in good habits." Bennett also quoted Aristotle the philosopher who posited that: "Good habits formed at youth make all the difference." [3]

Indelible and Unalterable

Plato, as far as the literature about him indicates, was not a confessed believer in God. And yet, his words about the importance of what young minds are exposed to syncs perfectly with the Christian philosophy of the importance of giving attention to the early training that a child receives. In his Socratic Dialogue (written about 352 B.C.), he spoke eloquently and profoundly about the importance of carefully screening the things that are fed into the minds of the young. In *The Republic, he* wrote:

> "You know the beginning is the most important part of any work, especially in the case of the young and the tender; for this is the time at which character is being formed and the desired impression is more readily taken. Shall we just carelessly allow children to hear any casual tales which may be devised by casual persons, and to receive into their minds ideas, for the most part, that are the very opposite of those which we should wish them to have when they are grown up?
>
> Anything received into the mind at that age is likely to become indelible and unalterable, and therefore, it is most important that the tales which the young first hear should be models of virtuous thoughts."[4]

Plato is clear that the early training of a child is of utmost importance, for a young child will indeed live what he or she learns. Learning is not limited to formal instruction or to a specific time or place. It happens 24/7 and in myriads of ways. Children have active mimic neurons in their brains and they will mimic what they behold, for it is another truism, that it is not so much what is taught, but what is caught. The human mind generally reflects the character of anything upon which it feeds. It is also a truism that we reap what we sow. For children to take these seven virtues and other necessary ones seriously, they must be in the presence of parents and other adults who also take them seriously. It has been said, "The society that molds you when you are young, stays with you for the rest of your life."

Our secular, postmodern society feeds our children a diet of immorality, skepticism, doubt, anti-God philosophies, violence, and vane entertainment. Is it any wonder that even young children are engaged in harming themselves, their peers, their family, and whoever is in sight, when the lines between reality and the virtual become blurred? An ancillary truism holds that "what we sow, we reap and what we reap we keep."

The Crucial Developmental Years

Jesus believed in, and practiced early childhood education. It was His custom and practice to invite young children to spend time with Him; He knew what He taught them would leave an indelible impression on their developing minds. Developmental psychologists, anthropologists, and educators have done a great deal of research on how the human mind and body function. They have documented the stages along the continuum of child development and have identified the optimum periods for learning and growth. They all agree that early child hood development is the basis of optimal human development.

Swiss developmental psychologist Jean Piaget is best known for his theory of child cognitive development. He believed that children developed knowledge in an organized way, each of which builds upon the earlier stages. The first four of the six stages and their predominant development skills are: (1) Sensory-motor Stage, from birth to approximately two years, characterized by the development of reflexes, coordination and trial and error experimentation; (2) Preoperational Stage, between two and six years, characterized by language development and the use of symbolism; (3) Concrete Operational Stage, from age seven to around 11, characterized by logical thinking; (4) Formal Operational Stage, from 12 to adulthood, characterized by the ability to think about abstract concepts. [5]

Although Piaget's theory is helpful in understanding how children learn, it is generally believed by modern developmental theorists that the stages of development in children are not as rigidly calibrated as Piaget first theorized. There is general agreement, however, that early childhood is the period between zero to eight years of age. This is the period of greatest growth and development, when the brain develops most rapidly, almost to its fullest. It's a period when walking, talking, self-esteem, visions of the world, and moral foundations are established.

Child development specialists generally agree that when a child is at the age of reasoning, from age two to seven, the brain acts like a sponge. He or she absorbs everything around them, consciously or subconsciously. Many child psychologists believe that it is during this time that parents must really watch how they behave. How the parents speak, act, or go about their daily chores will be absorbed by the child during these times. Even when the parents think their child is preoccupied with something else, the child is likely perceiving and absorbing everything around them.

Sally Shaywitz, co-director of the Yale Center for the Study of Learning and Attention, posits that: "The period between ages 4-6 is a time of very intense activity in the brain; the brain is actively pruning synapses—the connections between brain cells. As the child is exposed to different experiences in life, the brain reinforces some of these connections and prunes back others that are not going to be useful. The brain is becoming more focused and more specialized. It's taking shape."[6] The prime time to establish the foundation and set the trajectory of a child's life is from the very beginning of life, while the "concrete" of their lives is still wet.

Inherited or Acquired

Each spring as I plant my beans, I notice how the growing vines need no help climbing up the strings that I place among them for their support. They climb all the way down the row, because they have been programmed by nature to do just that. Children are not born with a naturally good nature that leads them to do the things that are noble and pure and right. They are born with an unfair disadvantage, for they are all born as fallen beings, and with a *strong* proclivity to do wrong. At birth they are devoid of all seven virtues presented in this book. They need to be programmed to learn what these virtues are, and be given guided practice in inculcating them into the central operating system of their minds and into the fabric of their beings. Parents must be intentional in engaging their children's attention and passion, in the things that are: "True ... noble ... right ... pure ... lovely ... admirable ... excellent or praiseworthy" (Philippians 4:8.)

Moral literacy is the compass and true GPS–God Positioning System–in a world that is infinitely more evil than it is minimally morally good. "Moral anchors and moorings have never been more necessary [than they are today]." The moral deterioration of the age is threatening to both parents and child. Our children must be nurtured to develop the gift of discernment–the ability to identify the content and forces of these virtues. For virtues not understood, and hence ignored, become vices.

Prime Time: The First Seven Years

The mind of a child is fertile ground for good or for evil. It was Francis Bacon who once said, "The fattest ground brings forth nothing but weeds, if it is not properly tilled." As an avid gardener, I have learned by experience that a plowed garden will produce nothing but weeds if it is not cultivated with the desired plants. It is the sacred responsibility of parents to cultivate the fertile mind of their child with the things of God and the values of His kingdom.

At birth, a child's brain contains over one hundred billion cells. After birth, the synapses and neurons in the brain begin a period of rapid activity so that before long, a child is able to crawl, laugh, walk, speak, remember, recognize, and so much more. This is nothing short of a miracle. The five senses of vision, hearing, smell, taste, and touch constitute the brain's sensory "computer" that will enable the child to experience the world in a personal way.

The first seven years of a child's life is prime time for both God and the devil. The devil places all children on the endangered species list. Even before the time of their birth, the forces of good and evil begin to wrestle for their souls. Parents must seize the malleable moment in their child's life and cooperate with God to nurture and develop spiritual champions, starting from the delicate moment of conception. Children, like eggs, must be handled with care; for children, once broken, like eggs once broken, are the hardest things to be repaired. Manufacturers of consumer products may recall their merchandise and retrofit them for defective parts, but children cannot be recalled and retrofitted. Parents have one chance to do it right, and if they do it right under God's leadership, once is enough. Early training of our children cannot be overemphasized.

> "Too much importance cannot be placed on the early training of children. The lessons that the child learns during the first seven years of life, have more to do with forming his character than all that it learns in future years ... The parents' work must begin with the child in infancy, that it may receive the right impress of character, ere the world shall place its stamp on mind and heart. It is during the first years of a child's life that his mind is most susceptible of impressions either good or evil. During these years, decided progress is made in either a right direction or a wrong one."[7]

The goal of this book is to provide a biblically-based set of eternal principles that should be taught to children by age seven. It is these principles that will largely determine how they live and where they will spend eternity. I am writing to you as a parent myself, and the seven virtues I will explore with you have been a part of my child rearing practice from the time my first child was born. You undoubtedly may choose to practice with, and help your child develop more than these seven virtues before age seven, but it is my belief that the seven virtues I will outline for you, are the foundation upon which all children can build a solid spiritual, moral, intellectual, physical and social life that honors their Maker and Savior. It is during these first seven crucial years that lifelong beliefs, attitudes, values and habits are formed, becoming attributes of a child's character.

Be mindful that the stronger the foundation, the stronger the building. As you prayerfully peruse the pages of this book, never forget that a weak building may stand on a strong foundation, but a strong building cannot stand on a weak foundation. Build your children from foundation up and they will be able to stand firm when the tests of life come to them. And come they will!

How to use This Book

It is undeniable that the world is changing rapidly and radically. I do not view the writing of this book as a mere opportunity. I regard it as a responsibility. As a former high school and elementary school principal, I have worked with children and parents long enough to know that something is very wrong in our society, and also that there is a spiraling decline in the embrace of moral values. This decline, I believe, is threatening the moral upbringing of today's children.

Culturally and morally, our society is long past the amber alert. The red flags are up, the red lights are flashing; our children are crashing morally. Johanna Michaelson, in her book, *Like Lambs to the Slaughter* writes: "We are raising a generation of children for whom there are no absolutes, no right or wrong, no morals, no allegiance to government or family. This generation of children is being groomed to believe that Christianity is a dead, empty, irrelevant religion that is bigoted and narrow-minded; a religion to be feared and despised, for it stands in the way of the New Age of harmony, and unity and peace."[8]

I write out of an anguished heart, because I see the life-threatening dangers that our children face, and, consequently, the even greater danger that lies ahead of them. This book on the *Seven Virtues to Teach Your Child by Age Seven*, is in no way exhaustive on the matter of what to teach our children during those crucial first seven years. There are a myriad of other virtues and beneficial things that we should also be teaching during this period of rapid development and delightful curiosity.

Each chapter will close with a summary of "how to" ideas. This will give you an opportunity to explore ways of making these development age-appropriate, practical, and God-honoring for your child. Use your creativity and imagination as you design and demonstrate age-appropriate lessons to introduce and mold these virtues into the mind and character of your child.

By design, the Word of God will be the main resource for this book, for none other is as instructive in its precepts, so ennobling in its principles, nor so transforming in its influence.

And do not forget: when it's age-appropriate, to always seek ways to explain to your child *what* your goal is and *how* attaining it will help to make the process of learning and development meaningful and fulfilling. Strategies for teaching these virtues must vary according to a child's maturity and level of comprehension. Quantity and quality time spent with children, especially in the days of their youth, is never wasted: "Sow your seed in the morning, and in the evening let not your hands be idle, for you do not know which will succeed, whether this or that, or whether both will do equally well." (Proverbs 11:6).

This book is for all those who raise children–parents, grandparents, parents to be, and teachers, of every political and religious persuasion, of every gender, race or creed. It is a book of instruction and resources for all those who will raise godly children for the kingdom of heaven and the glory of God.

It is my sincere prayer that God will open your heart to a new and deeper understanding and meaning about the joys and responsibilities of having and raising children for the only goal worth sacrificing everything for—eternal life. It is also my sincere prayer that the seven spiritual virtues discussed in this book, and more, will become habits of sanctifying grace-in-motion in your children as they grow and glow in grace.

The children are watching ... absorbing ...
mimicking ... watching you and me.
Be gentle, be kind, be careful what you do, for you
are, by example, making another you.

1

The Development of Godly Character

"Sons are a heritage from the Lord, children a reward from him."
(Psalm 127:3)

The development of godly character in their children is the first and most enduring task of God-honoring parenting. Planting godly virtues in the young takes precedence over all other parental responsibilities. No amount of earthly success in a parent's life will compensate for the loss of one child from the kingdom of God to the kingdom of Satan.

Parents are partners with God, walking with Him as they lead their children in the direction of heaven. Discovering and rediscovering the virtues and values of the kingdom of God will energize our children to "increase in wisdom and stature and in favor with God and man."[9] God delights in using children to display what the kingdom of heaven is like (Matthew 18:1-6), so why not facilitate our children coming to Jesus, their Friend and Savior, and in the process make them, indeed, heaven's best commercial: "Let the children come to me and do not forbid them for the kingdom of heaven belongs to such as these" (Matthew 19:14).

1

The virtues that I present in this book are, first of all, attributes and principles of the character of God. They are communicable attributes that can and should become character traits and attitudinal skills for all humankind to develop, learn, and emulate. Once learned, these virtues affect the way people think, feel, act, and live their lives. Contrary to what some people may think, virtues are not non cognitive skills. They do involve the engagement of the mind in order to learn them and make them an integral part of a person's conscious and intentional spiritual, mental, social, and emotional "operating system."

Before I expound on the seven virtues that parents should teach their children by age seven, it is imperative that I answer five fundamental questions: (1) Why should we desire children? (2) Who owns our children? (3) Why does God give us children? (4) What eternal plans does God have for our children? (5) And what is the divine design for educating our children?

But first, let me reinforce a well-known fact: Parents bear the lifelong, God-given responsibility for educating and caring for God's heritage. Mothers and fathers are responsible for the health, the physical and moral safety, and the development of the character of their children. This is a work that cannot be outsourced to others. God-honoring parents are in partnership with God to raise godly offspring.

Why Do We, or Should We, Desire Children?

Children are a gift from God (Psalm 127:3). The gift of procreation was given to humans from the very beginning–"Be fruitful and increase in number" (Genesis 1:26). It is God's delight when we have children who will fulfill His design for them. But the question still remains: Why do we, or should we, desire to have children? The story of Hannah and Samuel recorded in 1

Samuel 1:1-20, probably provides the quintessential biblical answer to this age-old question.

Elkanah, the son of Jeroham, had two wives. One of his wives (Penninah) was childbearing, and the other (Hannah) was childless. Not even a double portion of Elkanah's food could satisfy Hannah's emptiness of not having a child of her own. Hannah was provoked into bitter tears by her rival Peninnah, who had many sons and daughters of her own.

Hannah turned to the only one who could do anything about her barrenness and prayed: "O Lord Almighty, if you will only look upon your servant's misery and remember me, and not forget your servant but give her a son, then I will give him back to the Lord for all the days of his life (1 Samuel 1:11). Hannah's promise to the Lord to give her son back to Him *all* the days of his life *is* the purest reason why parents should desire to have children. God's gift to us of children should be given back to Him as a thankful and eternal gift to their Maker and Giver. Hannah's life story has taught all desiring parents two important parenting lessons: First, *ask* God for the gift of a child. And second, joyfully *give* that gift (from the day of conception) back to God.

Who Owns Our Children?

Our children come to us as the certified pre-owned heritage of God. They are certified, for they bear His image and stamp, trademarked by their Maker (Genesis 1:27). The psalmist is precise in who owns our children: "Sons are the heritage from the Lord, children a reward from Him (Psalm 127:3). God has the rights to our children, and parents have the responsibility for raising them for His glory. God is not the grand or great-great grandfather of our children. He *is* their Father. He made each one of them with His own hands: "For you created my inmost being; you knit me together in my mother's womb" (Psalm 139:13). At best, earthly parents are surrogate parents, inheriting from God the children that He made and owns.

Every child is a God-given sacred trust. Our children belong to God, their heavenly Father, by creation and redemption. They are entrusted to their earthly parents' care during the time between their birth and their death. God will ask for an accounting for His heritage. His design is that they spend eternity with Him some day. He is coming back to receive them unto Himself.

Why Does God Give Us Children?

God-honoring parenting is a purpose-driven activity. However, no matter how much we love our children, or no matter how well-intentioned we are about their best good, we will do an inadequate job of raising them. When God enables us to have children, He also provides the help we need to nurture them in the path of morality and righteousness. Until parents fully understand why God gave them children, it will be impossible for them to understand His design for their care, education, and destiny. Contrary to what many people think, children were not given to parents to be their security in a time of need. It is the other way around. Parents are the earthly security for their children. They owe it to their children to care for them, and not the other way around, for it was their parents' choice to bring them into existence. The quintessential text in the Bible that unmistakably clarifies God's design for His heritage is found in Malachi 2:15. It is worth studying this text in its context. Malachi was addressing the men of Israel on a very delicate subject—their marriage covenants with their wives. Then he asked them a poignant question: "Has not the Lord made them one? In flesh and spirit they are his. And why one? Because he was seeking *godly offspring* who are made in His image. So guard yourself in your spirit, and do not break faith with the wife of your youth" (Malachi 2:15; emphasis added).

God's purpose for giving us children constitutes a divine covenant with us. It simply states that the fruit of the womb, the children they bear, will be His, and that they should be raised as *godly* offspring. God-honoring parenting *is* a purpose-driven activity indeed! Its primary goal is to raise godly children who are God-fearing, spiritual, religious, righteous, reverent, moral, devout, and holy. Every child comes to his or her earthly parent with a conditional use permit (CUP). They must be raised and nurtured by parents according to God's design and eternal purpose. There is no scripture that says that children were given to parents so that they can make them into professionals—musicians, artists, scientists, sports stars, Olympians, etc. As noble as those goals may be, every child must be led to first and foremost become a godly offspring, seeking first the kingdom of God and His righteousness (Matthew 6:33). It will profit us as parents—and our children nothing—if they receive the best earthly education, achieve fame and wealth, and attain positions of power and prestige, if in the process of doing so, they did not become godly offspring.

Peter Marshall, a former chaplain of the United States Senate, once wrote, "If we are not raising godly offspring, we are simply raising pagans." Ouch! That hurts, but is it not the truth? No amount of success in one's life will compensate for missing the divine goal—godly offspring. Through the gift of procreation, God has given parents the supreme privilege of helping to populate His kingdom on earth and in heaven. Wow! It's a privilege that is not even given to angels. What a privilege indeed!

The gross domestic product (GDP) of a country is the sum total of all the goods and services that it provides. The GDP of the home is each godly offspring that it produces for the kingdom of heaven.

What Eternal Plans Does God Have for Our Children?

Human beings were created to live eternally. However, when the first couple chose to sin, they forfeited eternal life. This did not please God, since He created humans to have eternal fellowship with Him. Once the first couple sinned, God did not hesitate to redeem them and all those who would sin as a result of the fall. The "Lamb slain from the creation of the world" (Revelation 13:7) paid for humankind's redemption with His own death on the cross.

The choice to live eternally was temporarily lost in Eden, but it has been fully restored to all those who would be born after Adam and Eve. And that is why the scriptures confidently state, "He has made everything beautiful in its time. He has also set eternity in the hearts of men" (Ecclesiastes 3:11). Eternity has been planted in the hearts of our children even as they were being fashioned in the womb by the hands of God. Humanity's eternity was being "forefilled" in the Garden of Eden, and so was the eternal doom and destruction of Satan (Genesis 3:15).

God, the gracious and redeeming Father of all Israel (literally and spiritually), gives timeless priority to children and guarantees their physical and spiritual salvation in the powerful words spoken through Isaiah the prophet: "I will contend with those who contend with you, and your children I will save" (Isaiah 49:25b). When God saves His children physically, it is because He has plans to save them eternally also. Our children were made to live eternally with their Maker, and that is guaranteed through the redeeming love of Jesus their eternal Friend.

What is the Divine Design for educating our children?

The first priority of parents is to educate their children for heaven. "It must forever be heaven before Harvard," as one of my colleagues likes to say. God enjoins parents to train/educate their children: "Train a child in the way he should go, and when he is old he will not turn from it" (Proverbs 22:6). This is undoubtedly a widely debated text of Scripture, and there is a wide spectrum of interpretations about its meaning, but note that the text begins with a powerful verb, "train." To train is to educate, to shape, to focus on a goal or aim, to direct.

Parents are the first and most influential teacher of their children. That is exactly how God designed it, with a supreme purpose in mind—that the young would be raised and educated to become godly offspring. The quote from *Newsweek*, May 31, 2004, is worth repeating here: "No educational system, no matter how it is designed, can make up for that which is not given to children in their homes."

There are only two Bible-endorsed methods for educating our children—home school and church school. God Himself modeled home schooling. It was right there in the Garden of Eden that He educated Adam and Eve about their role in their perfect world. Right there He told them what to eat and what not to eat; how to manage the animals, and how to multiply and replenish the earth. Home schooling is a God-ordained educational strategy to provide the young with a correct and biblical worldview about their Creator and everything else of divine importance.

It was not God's plan to outsource the education of children. However, after the heads of families failed to do their work of educating their children, God directed Samuel to establish church schools—the Schools of the Prophets—to ensure that children would be instructed in His ways. In the beginning, home, school, and church were co-terminus—they shared the same space, and they were also co-curricular—the curriculum was the same in home, church, and school. They even shared the same parent/teacher/pastor—God. In the home-school and the church-school, the Word of God must be the foundation—the curriculum, the center and circumference of everything that children learn. Any educational system in the home, school or church that does not have the Word of God as its foundation should be off-limits to God's heritage. For such systems are in effect teaching everything about nothing and nothing about the things that mean everything. The godly learning environment of home-school and church school gives our children a true home-court advantage to have a winning record for Christ.

When parents outsource the education of their children to the ungodly, mockers, and the wicked (Psalm 1:1), they are simply employing the services of the anti-Christ (1 John 4:2) to produce rebellious children or lukewarm Christians, at best. Anything that disowns and dishonors God cannot benefit the souls of our children. If, as parents, we are not doing exactly what God requires of us, we are not doing His will at all. God's supreme blessings cannot attend those who knowingly violate His eternal principles of righteousness.

Many of the things that children will learn to do as they mature daily are self-emergent. They will learn to crawl, smile, walk, talk, and do a host of other tasks without being taught by anyone. They are hard-wired to do these things. However, they will not learn about God and the values of His kingdom, or develop the necessary spiritual, social, and vocational life-skills without being taught by someone. Parents are a child's first and most important teachers. They are God's representatives on earth to guide His heritage from the days of their youth, so that when they are older they will abide in His nurture and admonition. Raising godly children is neither a sprint nor a relay. It is a marathon from the womb to the tomb. There is no time off for parents!

The Virtues

Now that we have established the rationale for a proactive and purpose-driven approach to educating our children from birth, let me enumerate the seven virtues that are definitely *not* self-emergent, but must be taught with intentionality, persistence, and with one divine objective in mind—to produce godly offspring for the kingdom of God on earth and in heaven. The virtues are not presented in any prioritized order. In reality, they are most effectively developed when they are introduced into a child's life concurrently, by precept and example. Godly virtues are not self-emergent. They will not automatically become a part of our children's character. It is God's plan that parents and Godly adults and teachers will not only model kingdom values, but be the triggers that will begin the development of kingdom values in His heritage.

Because children are born spiritually damaged or depraved, it is necessary to build their characters by training them in the virtues and graces of Christ. It is through this training and guidance that parents will come to know the capabilities, inclinations, interests, strengths, and weaknesses of their children. Parenting is a comprehensive task and can only be done successfully with supernatural help from Him who is the embodiment of all wisdom and knowledge. Even as God has created each child with eternity in mind, so also must *parenting* begin with eternity in mind. For that is the true essence of anticipatory intelligence—allowing the destination (heaven) to influence and guide every decision and action along the journey of life. Anticipatory intelligence is, in essence, "remembering ahead"—keeping in mind the certainty of salvation that Christ has guaranteed for His heritage: "Your children I will save" (Isaiah 49:25).

Jesus lovingly invites our children to remember Him in the days of their youth, (Ecclesiastes 12:1) and through the words of the Psalmist, He envisions for them a glorious and prosperous future: "Our sons in their youth will be like well-nurtured plants, and our daughters will be like pillars carved to adorn a palace" (Psalm 144:12). If anyone can make this goal an exciting reality for parents, the sovereign God can. For when humanity is united with divinity, impossible things happen! So let's "Just do it!"

After the entrance of sin into the world and the resulting corrupting and deadly pathology of paternity during the patriarchal era, God sought for a way to communicate His love and His will to the families of the earth, since the heads of the families had failed to do so. It was during this time that God commended Abraham for his parenting style and success in leading his family to godly living. By precept and example, Abraham was able to command his children and household after himself, directing them in the way of the Lord and helping them to do what was right and just (Genesis 18:19).

Can God count on us, as parents, to raise and lead our children by precept and example to honor God through godly living? Like Hannah, will we give our children back to God from the days of their youth for His service and glory?

2

The First Virtue
Reverence

"Since we have these promises dear friends, let us purify ourselves
from everything that contaminates body and spirit,
perfecting holiness out of reverence for God."
(2 Corinthians 7:1)

Reverence for God is the beginning of a sanctified life of purity
and holiness. The true story is told of a man called Daniel. Daniel
was a trusted advisor of kings Nebuchadnezzar and Darius. Daniel
knew God personally, for he respected and reverenced Him from the
days of his youth. His reverence for this God led him to bow down
and worship Him three times daily. This act of reverence for, and
worship to God made enemies of Daniel's fellow advisors. The king's
nobles and wise men did not like the fact that Daniel worshiped
another God—the God of heaven. So they devised a plan to do him
harm and to possibly put him to death.

These conniving nobles tricked King Darius into establishing a
law requiring that for 30 days, no one should be seen worshiping or
praying to any other god but Darius. Anyone who disobeyed would
be put to death. The vane and egocentric king quickly agreed to

the inviolable law. Daniel knew that the law was passed. However, he continued his daily routine of worship and prayer to the God of heaven. Before long, he was reported to the king. The king loved Daniel. Very unwillingly, he sent for Daniel and ordered that he be thrown into the den of hungry lions. "Perhaps, your God whom you serve so faithfully will save you from the lions." (Daniel 6:1-28)

The king went home but was so depressed that he could not eat or sleep. The following day he went to the lions' den to check on his distinguished advisor, Daniel. When he called out for him, he was scarcely hoping to hear a response. But from the darkness of the lions' den came the voice of Daniel: "O king, live forever, my God sent His angels and He shut the mouths of the lions. They have not hurt me" (Daniel 6:21:22). The king was happy that Daniel was alive. He ordered his guards to remove him from the lions' den and sent out a new decree to his province: "I issue a decree that in every part of my kingdom people must fear and reverence the God of Daniel, for he is the living God and he endures forever; his kingdom will not be destroyed, his dominion will never end" (Daniel 6:26).

Daniel reverenced and worshiped God, and God honored and rescued him. The call to reverence God is not an *advice* or a *suggestion*. It is a divine imperative with a choice—I will or I won't. And those who choose to reverence the Almighty God *will* be honored by Him. The truth of God about the values of His kingdom and the virtues of His character are on a collision course with the values of an anti-God society. But truth is its own judge. The truth of God wins the duel with falsehood every time.

Biblical Reverence

It is most appropriate to establish the context for understanding the virtue of reverence by going to the Word of God. No one says it better than the psalmist in Psalms 95:3-7. He powerfully declares the rationale for giving reverence to God: "For the Lord is the great God, the great king above all gods. In his hands are the depths of the earth, and the mountain peaks belong to Him. The sea is his, for he made it, and his hands formed the dry land. Come, let us bow down in worship, let us kneel before the Lord our Maker; for he is our God, and we are the people of his pasture, the flock under his care."

Reverence for God is the seed of holiness. It is the foundational cornerstone for building a trusting, grace-filled, and enduring relationship with Him. Reverence for God is the spiritual oxygen of the soul. It is the spiritual, life-energizing, divine nutrient that nourishes each child to grow as Jesus did, "increasing in wisdom and stature, and in favor with God and man" (Luke 2:52). Reverence for God leads a child to know who God is experientially and mystically. It is the spiritual GPS (God positioning system) that starts a child out in life with a biblical worldview instead of a secular one. It accurately documents each person's relationship with God–where they stand, with Him or against Him. Reverence for God is the anchor that keeps a child connected to his or her Maker. Reverence introduces a child to the cardinal variable that will determine where he spends eternity–with God or without Him.

Let's dissect the word, "reverence" and take a close look at its "anatomy and physiology"–its make-up and function–as it relates to the spiritual, mental, physical and social development of a child. The word "reverence" is from the Hebrew word, "shaw-khaw" and it means to prostrate, bow down, worship or give homage to royalty or to God. *The American Heritage Dictionary* defines reverence as: "A feeling of profound awe and respect, love, and veneration." To show reverence to God means more than to bow or curtsy. It means to acknowledge that He is Sovereign and the only One deserving of our unwavering devotion, adoration, praise, and worship.

Declaration of God's Holiness

The holiness of God is not a foreign theme to the occupants of heaven—the un-fallen angels. Isaiah 6:1-3 records a vision that the prophet had of a worship scene in the courts of heaven. Isaiah's report of his vision speaks volumes about the holiness of God. He saw God high and exalted and His train filled the temple. He also saw the seraphs as they covered their faces and their feet as they passed before the Holy God. And as these heavenly beings passed before God, Isaiah heard them calling out: "Holy, holy, holy is the Lord Almighty; the whole earth is full of His glory" (Isaiah 6:3).

Bible-believing Christians acknowledge the Holy God as the Creator and Redeemer of the world. These two realities alone (Creator and Redeemer) set God infinitely above all man-made gods. From the very beginning, God saw that sinful man was prone to serve gods of his own making. So He gave specific commands about how He should be related to—respected and reverenced. In giving the Ten Commandments to Moses, God established His Sovereignty and holiness in the first three: You must have no other gods before me … do not make or bow down to any graven image … and do not misuse the name of God, for no one will be guiltless for misusing His name (Exodus 20: 3-7).

As the Children of Israel travelled from Egypt to Canaan, God would appear to Moses for consultation, but never was Moses privileged to see God's face, for "un-holiness" cannot dwell with holiness. God provided, through Moses, moral, ceremonial and civil laws that should guide the people. He even provided guidelines about how the people should wash, dress, and prepare their bodies before coming to the place of worship to meet with Him.

The Fear of the Lord

Solomon, the greatest king of Israel, made repeated calls to people in every generation to "fear God." The expression, "fear

God," is not a call to be afraid of Him. It is a call to give reverence to God for Who He is: Creator, Redeemer, Comforter, and King of kings. As a child progresses from the infant years to adulthood, his or her knowledge of the world and how it functions will increase. Solomon's call to "fear God" is a confirmation that the only way that a child can "increase in wisdom [knowledge] and stature, and in favor with God and man," is to *begin* that process of growth with true reverence for Who God is. Therefore, there is no better time to teach a child to reverence God, than at the very beginning of life when his or her mind and heart are most impressionable. And is it not true that if we are not raising reverent children, we are only raising captives and servants of the devil? As harsh as the forgoing statement sounds, there are no two ways about it!

True Reverence

There are two masters in the world–God, the rightful Master and King, and Satan, the usurper and counterfeiter. The forces of good and evil are constantly at war, contending to gain the allegiance of every child that is born, and this war will not cease until Jesus returns to receive His heritage into His kingdom. Satan is the ultimate strategist. When he wants to get at parents he gets after their children, for he knows how emotionally wrapped up parents are in their children.

One of the great victories of Satan in modern times is that he has convinced many parents that there is no war going on over the minds of their children or that there are only "war games" in progress and not a real war. Parents therefore, let down their guards and Satan has his way with their children, and ultimately with them. The parental attitude that denies that there is a war being waged for their children's minds shows a lack of consequential intelligence–to every "to every action there is a reaction." Parents must be vigilant and intentional about teaching their children to serve one master only–God–and to give their allegiance to none other but the Sovereign God who made them and has redeemed them. "True reverence for God is inspired by a sense of His infinite greatness and a realization of His presence. With this sense of the Unseen the heart of every child should be deeply impressed."[10]

Our children are growing up in a secular and hostile environment– a culture that is anti-Creator God, Christ-rejecting, and devil-dominated. Parents can no longer afford to be passive about what their children learn, and who become their master and their primary influence. "Awelessness" and lawlessness are cooperating forces that threaten to enslave our children and detour them from the path of righteousness into a path of God-less, pleasure-seeking, self-serving, dead-end journey. God-honoring and gospel-powered parenting demands that parents become proactive in cultivating the minds of their children and planting in them the knowledge of who God is, and what His plans are for their eternal salvation.

In the beginning, man was created with an inherent, holy and reverential respect for God. Adam and Eve knew that God was their Maker. They knew that He was righteous and holy. When they chose to sin, the first thing they did when God came down to commune with them, was to hide. They knew that their relationship with Him was damaged or destroyed, and that in their unrighteousness, they could not meet Him face to face. True reverence for God is the conscience of the soul. It informs the soul when it is out of alignment with the holiness of the sovereign God.

God-Centered or Child-Centered

William Farley, in his book, *Gospel-Powered Parenting*, declares that; "Effective parents are not child-centered. They are God-centered. They strive to put God at the center of their family."[11] The *modus operandi* of our postmodern culture is all about *raising* children rather than *educating* them. Farley's declaration about God-centered parenting may seem like child abuse to postmodernists, but it is not. It is his call to parents to give God His rightful place in their homes, for when He is thus respected and reverenced, it will make all the difference in how each member of the family relates to their Maker and to each other. A wise sage once said: "You have to give it to modern parents: they know how to obey their children, even above obeying God." Parents are called to fear God and not their children.

Happy the Child

Children who learn to reverence God from the days of their youth are endowed with the most important relationship-building virtue that will lead to a personal and growing friendship with their Maker. True reverence for the omnipresent, omniscient, and omnipotent God will keep a child walking in the right direction—in the path of righteousness and toward God. Reverence in the heart gives rectitude to the life. "Happy the child, who by trust, submission and reverence toward his earthly protectors, learns to trust and obey and reverence his God. He who imparts to child or pupil such a gift has endowed him with a treasure more precious than the wealth of all the ages—a treasure as enduring as eternity."[12] Reverence for God gives wisdom and wisdom gives protection, exaltation, honor, grace, crown of splendor, guidance, and a steady walk with God (Proverbs 1:7; 4:5-12).

A Powerful and Enduring Lesson about Reverence for God

Someone has aptly said, "The predominant religion of the postmodern world is confusionism' that leads to twistianity'—confusion about: what is true and what is false, what is right and what is wrong, what is good and what is bad." "Twistianity" is a spinoff of "Christianity." Is it any wonder that "truth-ache" and "truth-decay" are so prevalent even among believers today? Our postmodern world extols a culture where everything "just is"– nothing is right or wrong, good or bad, sacred or common. However, Bible-believing Christians must teach their children that there are absolutes–right and wrong, good and evil, and sacred and common. At one point in the history of Israel as God's chosen people, God instructed Aaron the priest: "You must distinguish between the holy and the common, between the clean and the unclean, and you must teach the Israelites all the decrees the Lord has given them through Moses" (Leviticus 10:10).

Eli, the priest of Israel, had two sons–Hophni and Phinehas. They served alongside their father in the temple of the Lord but they treated the sacred things of God with contempt. They polluted the priesthood by their greed and immoral conduct. Eli, their father, did not restrain them and so all three of them died tragically within a short period of time, showing God's disapproval of their irreverence and contempt. (I Samuel 5:17, 18). Reverence for God and the sacred things of the Divine *is* serious business!

The By-Products of Reverence: Collateral Virtues

A life of reverence to God inspires: (a) a life of communication with God through His Word and through prayer; (b) a life of obedience to God; (c) and a life of grateful surrender to His will–all what I call collateral virtues.

A life of prayer: The act of praying to a Sovereign God is acknowledgement and acceptance that this God is worthy of our worship and also of being King of our lives. When the seed of reverence is sown in the heart of the young, and is nourished by a life of communing with Him through prayer and the study of His Word, such heart will grow into the full restoration of the image of God in man–increasing daily "in wisdom and stature and in favor with God and man." [13]

"Gentle Jesus meek and mild, look upon a little child; Pity my simplicity; Suffer me to come to Thee ..."[14] I frankly do not remember the first prayer that I learned as a child, but this was the first one that I taught my little children. However, long before they could utter words, I prayed for them, over them, and with them. My children came into the world in answer to prayers. I asked God for children who would honor His name.

Parents cannot give what they do not have. Children are perceptive and are far more intuitive than we credit them to be. They know when we are telling them to do something that we do not practice. It is difficult for parents to teach lifestyle practices to their children when their hearts do not embrace those practices. It *is* a truism that children live what they learn.

A life of obedience to God: Paul, the Apostle, asks the right and poignant question of all believers: "Don't you know that when you offer yourselves to someone to obey him as slaves, you are slaves to the one whom you obey—whether you are slaves to sin, which leads to death, or to obedience, which leads to righteousness?" (Romans 6:16). One of the supreme goals of every believer should be to become a voluntary slave to God, their Maker. Because reverence for God leads us to acknowledge His sovereignty, obedience to Him becomes the only intelligent choice we could/should make. This life of obedience to the Creator God leads to a life of moral righteousness and redemptive wholeness, thus guiding our children in the path of God's design—to become godly offspring.

A life of grateful surrender to His will: Surrender to God is not an easy virtue for anyone. However, Satan makes surrender to him attractive and easy. He is at his same old trick again: "You will not surely die" (Genesis 3:4). The natural tendency of the human heart is to be in control, to be in charge, to exercise power and authority over others, while at the same time resisting control over its life by anyone.

Reverence for God may not make surrender to His will *easy*, but it is the starting point of making it *possible* for God to be at the control center of our lives. Lucifer rebelled in heaven when he refused to surrender to the authority of God. He was cast out of the divine abode. Adam and Eve did the very same thing when they rebelled against God's provision for their eternal life. The history of the earth is punctuated with men and women who have rebelled against God's Sovereignty. And the consequences are always dire.

Surrender to God is more than a nice thing for our children. It is an imperative for anyone who desires to spend eternity with the God who is indisputably above all other gods. When children learn reverence for God, a life of prayer, obedience, and surrender become their godly passion and their life's ambition.

A life of biblical morality: Reverence for God will manifest itself in a life of purity, morality, and integrity. "Who may ascend into the hill of the Lord? Or who may stand in His holy place? He who has clean hands and a pure heart ... he shall receive blessing from the Lord, and righteousness from the God of his salvation" (Psalm 24:3-5). Biblical morality is a virtue that is honored and rewarded by God. It is taught in both Old and New Testament and modeled by Jesus when He lived as man among men.

Irreverence for God comes with an innumerable array of "collateral vices." Sexual immorality is a vice that is prevalent in our society. Children are constantly bombarded by not only sexual innuendos but explicit sex in the media, from which too many are not being shielded. The pressure on children to engage in sexual practices even before their bodies are fully developed is enormous. The Bible entreats our children to live moral lives by fleeing from sexual immorality (1 Corinthians 6:18) and by taking heed to the Word of God (Psalm 119:9). True reverence for a Holy God will serve as an effective barrier against immorality.

HOW TO TEACH REVERENCE

It is always good to remember that when raising godly offspring, it is not so much what is *taught* but what is *caught* that is of greatest importance and makes the most lasting impact. Teach age-appropriate reverence from the day of a child's birth.

- Teach by precept and example. The children are watching and mimicking
- Respect children and they will respect us and the God we represent
- Introduce children to the holiness of God
- Treat God's Name with reverence at all times
- Read and reread stories (the stories of Samuel, Daniel, Esther, Joseph) then talk with children about respect and reverence for God
- Teach children the difference between the sacred and the common
- Obey God's Word and His instruction for holy living
- Teach children to pray and to trust the Sovereignty of God
- Lead children to the family altar to bow down and commune with God daily
- Eliminate gaps between what God asks us to do and what we actually do
- Create a God-centered family where God's Word is the standard of living and guide in everything spiritual and secular
- Create opportunities for children to share their love for God in and out of the family circle
- Teach children to honor Christ in the choices they make– the things they choose to behold and eat; the places they choose to go; the music they choose to listen; the games they choose to play; and those whom they choose as friends. Educate children only in an environment where God and His Word are honored
- Praise and reinforce every act of reverence by expressing acknowledgement and approval.

- **FAMILY ACTIVITY:** Discuss, document, and practice more ways in which you can teach the virtue of reverence to children.

SUMMARY

Parents create the atmosphere in the home—a spiritual or a secular atmosphere—an atmosphere that reverences God or one that dishonors Him. The atmosphere in the home will shape the worldview of the child, leaving him or her with a biblical or secular one. It is a truism that, so the parent, so the home, and so the children. We do reap what we do sow! In raising godly offspring, reverence for God is a "PG"--rated activity for children. Parental guidance from day one is a divine imperative.

The proverbial three "R's" of "reading, 'riting, and 'rithmetic" are important for children to learn indeed. But for God-honoring parents, the fourth "R"—reverence—trumps them all. This reverence for God is the root of spirituality. It is this root that gives nourishment to a dynamic prayer life, a life of obedience to God, and a lifestyle of complete surrender to His will. This is the recipe for the making of a spiritual champion. Children *will* live what they learn and learn what they live. Do not let your children start life or leave home without it—reverence for God their Creator. Collateral virtues and collateral vices are constantly at war in our children, and God-honoring parents must do everything possible to help their children win this war.

3

The Second Virtue
Obedience

"Even a child is known by his actions,
by whether his conduct is pure and right."
(Proverbs 20:11)

Obedience to parents is a virtue that comes with a promised blessing from the Lord. God blesses obedience! Always! I once heard a story about twin brothers (Jaime and Johnny) who were always very competitive. When they were eight years old, they went on a trip to spend Spring break with their grandpa. To their delight, grandpa took them out on his tractor to feed the cows and plow the fields for planting corn. He then taught the boys how to plant the corn–three grains in each hole about twelve inches apart. Each boy was given a bag of corn and a small hand shovel and they enthusiastically set out to plant their corn.

It was not long before Jaime noticed that his brother was keeping up with him with the planting, so he devised a plan to finish his bag of corn ahead of his brother Johnny. Jaime started to place five grains of corn in each hole and at intervals of about two feet apart. Before long, his bag of corn was finished and he felt the thrill of "beating" his brother to the finish line again. "Grandpa, I just work fast and that's why I always finish my chores ahead of Johnny." His grandpa replied: "Jaime, these will take about seven days to sprout so you should be able to see the work of your hand before returning to home to mom and dad." A very sad Johnny had to work on for several more minutes until his bag of corn was all planted with the right amount of grains in each hole and at the right interval.

The following week, before the boys' parents came to retrieve them, grandpa took the boys out to the field to see if the corn had sprouted. Grandpa did not like what he saw. There was something unusual with the row of corn that Jaime planted. Instead of three growing buds, there were five coming out of each hole and at intervals of about two feet apart. "Jaime, is this the row of corn that you planted?" "Yes grandpa." "See anything unusual about it?" Jaime was silent! "Now I know why you finished ahead of your brother when you were planting last week." "Why, grandpa?" "Because you did not *obey* my instructions, you planted your corn five to a hole and 24 inches apart." "Now, Jaime, because you disobeyed my instructions, you sit here and think about your disobedience and dishonesty, while Johnny and I ride the tractor to fetch the hay and feed the cows. And when I return, I want you to tell me what you have learned from what you did."

Obedience: A Learned Virtue

The story of the Bible from Genesis to Revelation is a story about obedience. Obedience is God's language of love. Adam and Eve were invited to obey their Maker (Genesis 2:16-17), and the principal characteristic of the saints when Christ returns will be their obedience to Him (Revelation 14:12). Obedience is a learned virtue. The first sin that was committed in the universe was disobedience/rebellion—the refusal of Lucifer to submit to the authority of God. Since that fateful day, all humans have been infected with the deadly germ of rebellion and disobedience. In the final analysis, when Jesus returns for His chosen people, only those who willingly and obediently submit to His authority will be privileged to live with Him eternally.

No parent of a newborn (and specifically of a two-year-old) needs to be reminded that obedience is not an innate virtue. Even before children learn to speak, they begin to assert their independent will and are able to let their parents know that they are *not* ready to be obedient in everything. Like teaching a child how to play a musical instrument, teaching obedience must begin early in life. It must be patiently, consistently, and lovingly introduced, enforced, reinforced, rewarded, and celebrated. Teaching the virtue of obedience will call for "tough love" from parents. Discipline does not break a child's spirit half as much as it breaks a parent's heart. Parents are called upon by God to be parents and not just friends of their children. Children learn how to emotionally manipulate their parents even from the time they are in the crib. They can use emotionally manipulation effectively to have it their way instead of doing it the right way.

Teaching obedience is a team activity—with mother and father in agreement about what is acceptable behavior. Children are quick to play one parent against the other as soon as they realize that each has different standards for obedience.

Children are created in "the image of their Maker"—with the gift of creativity, reasoning, speech, self-determination, and choice. Every child is created with the ability to express love, kindness, forgiveness, and faithfulness (Exodus 34:6).

Often, the problem in teaching the virtue of obedience to children lies not with the children but with the parents. If fathers and mothers are not in control of their own attitudes and actions, will they be able to teach their children to be in control of their own attitudes and actions? Parental delinquency in living Godly values and in managing their children can lead to juvenile delinquency.

Respect for Authority

Fathers and mothers are called upon by God to take responsibility for the education of their young ones. Parenting is a God-given authority to represent Him in the home while planting the seed of "Godness" in their children. It seems that rebellion against authority is at a pandemic stage in every civilization. Whether it is against the authority of the sovereign God, the government, or of the home, people are in a state of revolt (Admittedly, it is not always a bad thing to revolt against an unjust government).

It is an undeniable truth of life that all human beings are answerable to someone else, whether it is in the home, in the work place, in society, or to God. The increasing informality in our culture has left us with a generation of cynics, who not only question authority, but disrespect it. The postmodern culture has cultivated a generation of children who have succeeded in infecting their seniors with their disdain for rules. These children, it would seem, are now teaching their parents and elders how to act. Allan Bloom, in his best-selling book, *The Closing of the American Mind*, put it poignantly: "You have to give it to American parents–they know how to obey their children."[15]

As politically incorrect as it may sound, parental authority is not what it used to be. The systematic de-parenting (taking away the rights of parents to discipline or even spank their children) of our society did not happen overnight. Inside and outside of the family, respect for authority has been replaced by transactional analysis–you are O.K. and I am O.K. The interpretation of rules has become highly individualized with personalized interpretation of what is right or wrong as the acceptable standard. The Bible teaches that heaven will be a place where people obey God and submit to His authority.

Obedience will not be taught or developed in heaven. God has made it clear that His followers are people who choose to obey Him while they are still on earth. If we love Him we will find delight in obeying His will on earth (Psalm 40:8). Children who cannot respect the authority of their parents will most likely not respect the authority of anyone else, not even the authority of God. Children will test parental authority, but such tests must be met with kindness and yet firmness. Jesus cares for all children—the best behaved as well as those who have objectionable character traits.

Obedience: a Heart/Belief Problem

All humans are born as genetically-modified organisms (GMO)—with a congenital heart defect. Physically, a child may be a picture of health at birth, cuddly and beautiful with all the essential organs intact and working efficiently. But what is not seen at birth is the DNA of the sinful nature that imprints the heart and mind. The sinful imprint on a child's heart will eventually grow into disobedience and rebellion. Reverence for God, goodness, obedience, and kindness are not self-emergent from the heart, for "a bad tree cannot bear good fruits" (Matthew 7:18).

Jeremiah posed the operative question about the inherited depravity of man's heart: "The heart is deceitful above all things, and desperately wicked. Who can know it?" (Jeremiah 17:9). Teaching obedience must begin at the heart of the problem—in the heart! Our children can only receive a new heart that is inclined to obey their parents and their God when they receive a spiritual heart transplant from the Divine Cardiologist Himself. This extreme-makeover of the human heart and mind is the only answer to the natural spirit of rebellion that a child is born with, and that manifests itself even from the days when that child is confined to his crib or his parent's arms.

As a gardener, I have learned to not transplant my tomato plants when they already have young tomatoes on them. The time to transplant them is when they are still young with the ability to establish a strong root system, before they begin to bear fruit. The spiritual heart transplant in children is no different. For maximum effect, it must be done at the earliest possible stage in their development. Once our children are born, the Devil loses no time in making them his prime targets. He begins to work on their will and to sow the evil seed of selfishness, disobedience, and intemperance. From the earliest age, parents must be intentional in sowing the good seeds of godly virtues in the tender garden-hearts of their children.

Biblical Discipline

Discipline is not a negative word as many people think. To discipline someone simply means to train that person to develop the desired competencies and habits that will have a positive effect on their life. The *American Heritage Dictionary* defines discipline as: "Training expected to produce a specific character or pattern of behavior." This definition makes it easy to understand the command of God to discipline our children when He instructed parents to: "Train a child in the way he should go, and when he is old he will not turn from it" (Proverbs 22:6). God is not in the business of giving advice or making suggestions. Because He is the all-knowing God, He gives directives, obedience to which will always result in the best for His heritage. Training is discipline and discipline is training. And it is all positive.

In teaching obedience to children, it is always better to request than to command. Obedience is best taught to children through the biblical discipline plan. Children will always make mistakes, and therefore should be treated with kindness and compassion at all times. Excessive rigidity in discipline is just as damaging as excessive permissiveness. Biblical discipline is God's plan for informing, transforming, and redeeming fallen humanity. It is founded in love, order, authority, and consistency. The Bible enjoins children to be respectful of parental authority and to obey their parents in the Lord: "Honor your mother and father which is the first commandment with promise that it may go well with you and that you may enjoy long life on earth. Children, obey your parents in the Lord, for this is right" (Ephesians 6:1, 2). A fundamental imperative of discipline is respect for the authority of parents.

Discipline has become a politically and emotionally sensitive word in our postmodern world, for no one seems to want to give it or receive it. Is it not true that when we refuse to correct our children or someone we love, it probably is because we have given up on them?

The Object of Discipline

"Parental authority isn't what it used to be. Parents are no longer eager to be parents. They want to love and guide their children as a trusted friend."[16] Our permissive and law-rejecting society may have varying ideas about the necessity of discipline and the objective for disciplining our children. However, the Bible is very clear that, "A child left to himself will bring shame to his mother" (Proverbs 29:15). Translation: An undisciplined child will not only bring disgrace to his or her parents, but will probably also bring destruction upon themselves. "One of the first lessons that a child needs to learn is the lesson of obedience. Before children are old enough to reason, they may be taught to obey. By gentle, persistent effort, the habit should be established. The object of discipline is the training of the child for self-regulation and self-government."[17] Teenage rebellion and juvenile delinquency are not overnight phenomena, which suddenly overtake our children. The seeds of such anti-social behaviors were sown from the days of infancy, and were probably nurtured by a lack of consistent training and discipline by the family. Self-government does not grow by in-grafting. It grows from seed only–the seed of obedience cultivated in the heart from the day of birth.

Ponder for a while, these powerful words:

> Every child that is not prayerfully and carefully disciplined will be unhappy. Children who are allowed to have their own way cannot be happy. The

un-subdued heart has not within it the elements of
rest and contentment. The mind and heart must be
disciplined and brought under proper restraint in
order for the character to harmonize with the laws
that govern our being. Restlessness and discontent
are fruits of indulgence and selfishness.[18]

Self-Government and Temperance

Temperance is a must-have virtue for believers who are
"increasing in wisdom and stature and in favor with God and man."
Temperance can be defined as moderation in the use of anything
that is good, and restraint from the use of anything that is not good
for body, soul, and mind. Children will not always be around parents
or others who will act as their conscience to make good choices for
them. Without self-government, children will act without restraint
and make choices that will negatively impact the health of body,
soul, and mind. The Apostle Paul makes it clear that anyone who is
striving for the mastery [spiritual maturity] is temperate in all things
(1 Corinthians 9:25). An undisciplined child will be intemperate
in the use and abuse of things that are good or bad. And that will
definitely affect his or her relationship with God and individuals.

Designer Discipline Direct from Genesis

Training/discipline should be designed to match the specific needs
of those being nurtured. That is, the rules, rewards and consequences
should apply directly to those who are being trained for self-
management. The virtues of obedience and self-management are like
the foundation of any building. If the foundation is solidly built, the
building on top of it will stand. A disobedient and undisciplined child
soon becomes a wrecking ball that destroys not only his own life, but
the lives of the people in his path also—all throughout his or her life.

The most effective training/disciplinary plan ever conceived was developed by God right there in the Garden of Eden, even before sin entered the purity of His creation. It is a disciplinary plan that transcends time and is still very effective today, when it is properly understood and applied.

During the research and soul searching in preparation for writing this book, a delightful serendipitous phenomenon happened. I discovered a plan for godly, designer discipline right there in the Scriptures. I call this biblical plan of designer discipline "OSIE-CER," pronounced "Ozie-sir." Stay with me now, for OSIE-CER is just an acronym for a revolutionary disciplinary design that is found in Genesis—the first book of the Bible. It is a plan that I guarantee will work wonders for young families. I am so sure of its effectiveness that I present it here as a money-back guarantee! God designed OSIE-CER for a perfect couple in a perfect home—Eden. However, this same method of training and discipline works beautifully with imperfect people in an imperfect world.

The seven-step OSIE-CER disciplinary plan is divided in two parts. Although the whole initiative is administered by the authority in charge—the parent—the first four steps (OSIE), require the initiative or response of the child, and the second three steps (CER) require the initiative or response of the authority—the parent.

The Promise and Power of OSIE-CER

Children need guidance from their parents in order to learn self-control and responsibility. I believe it was no coincidence that even as children were introduced into their Eden home, God modeled this kind of guidance for the new couple. The OSIE-CER training plan begins with God's power to create, and ends with His power to redeem. The principles of OSIE-CER are universal; they work across cultures, regardless of age; they work in the home, school, church, work place, and wherever people need to be trained, managed, disciplined, and rewarded. It is both preventive and redemptive.

We find this seven-step plan embedded in the story of the first week of creation that is recorded in Genesis 1-3. It was good for a sinless pair and now equally good for sinful people. Notice that the OSIE-CER method of training and discipline did not come as a reaction by God to the fall of man. It was given *before* sin while Adam and Eve were still in their perfect state.

- **(O) Order:** The first thing God did as He began the creative process was to create **order** and eliminate chaos on the earth, for: "The earth was formless and empty, darkness was over the surface of the deep, and the Spirit of God was hovering over the waters" (Genesis 1:1). Order is basic to any effective training/discipline plan. Order as a cardinal virtue is discussed in detail in the next chapter.

- **(S) Standard:** God then set the standard for how everything in His creation was going to be. His first act of creation was the creation of light. "Let there be light and there was light. God saw that the light was <u>good</u>" (Genesis 1:3, emphasis mine). Nothing that God does can be bested by Him or anyone else, for God is perfect and so is everything that He does. God's **standard** for all of the rest of creation and for everything that He does is "good." Divine excellence is an attribute of God and an ideal that He holds for all of His creation. From the very beginning, God's ideal for His children has been "higher than the highest human thought can reach." It is also important to note that God made light right at the start of creation, for plants and animals would need it for growth and development, and mankind for vision and guidance.

- **(I) Instructions:** After God had declared everything that He created "good," He then gave man **instructions** about how to live and care for the rest of creation. God's instructions provided clarity for Adam and Eve, so there would be no misunderstanding about how to enjoy their emerging eternal life: "Be fruitful and increase in number. Fill the earth and subdue it. Rule over the fish of the sea, the birds of the air, and over every living creature. I give you every seed-bearing plant ... they will be yours for food" (Genesis 1:29-30). Clear, courteous communication and instructions are necessary for any training/discipline plan to work effectively.

- **(E) Expectations**: God was careful to outline His expectations for righteous living to Adam and Eve. At creation, they enjoyed conditional eternal life. Their obedience to God's instructions and adherence to His **expectations** would extend their life into eternity: "And the Lord God commanded the man, 'You are free to eat from any tree in the garden; but you must not eat from the tree of the knowledge of good and evil, for when you eat of it you will surely die'" (Genesis 2:16-17). Like any good parent would do, God might have repeated His expectation to Adam, so that he was clear on what His Maker was asking of him. Divine expectations cannot be trifled with.

- **(C) Consequences**: Good consequences (rewards) must follow obedience, and negative consequences (punishment) must follow disobedience. Defiance must not be allowed to take root in the hearts of children. Consequences are both powerful lessons and master teachers. When people are shielded from the consequences of their disobedience they are being reinforced to keep repeating those behaviors, to their detriment. God was very clear to Adam about the consequences of disobedience to His rule/expectation: " ... for when you eat of it you will surely die." A good training/discipline plan will clearly outline the **consequences** for good or unacceptable behavior. After six millennia of human history on the earth, the wages of sin and disobedience is still death (Romans 6:23). There is a built-in consequence for disobedience.

- **(E) Enforcement:** Someone has said, "The surest way to make it hard for your children is to make it soft for them." True discipline is founded upon tough love. It must have pained the heart of God to enforce upon Adam and Eve the consequences of their disobedience, but out of love for them and the generations to follow, He had to: "To the woman He said, 'I will greatly increase your pains in childbearing ... your husband will rule over you'" (Gen 3:16). And to Adam God said, "Cursed is the ground because of you ... by the sweat of your brow you will eat food ... until you return to the ground" (Genesis 3:17-19). Rules without **enforcement** are useless. The human nature will soon learn to ignore any rule that is not enforced. Children, in particular, are quick to discern when enforcement of a rule is either sporadic or non-existent. The sooner children are allowed to face the consequences of their actions, the sooner they will learn the true object of discipline–self management.

- **(R) Redemption:** Redemptive discipline gives the offender an opportunity to re-establish a relationship of obedience and to come into a position of realignment with authority. Redemptive discipline is an initiative of the one who is offended. God initiated redemption of Adam and Eve and all succeeding generations when He declared to them and to the Devil: "I will put enmity between you and the woman, and between your offspring and hers. He will crush your head and you will strike his heal (Genesis 3:15). In this crucial step, God sets the standard for what true redemptive discipline should be–the *offended* must initiate the redemptive process. When children have violated family rules, and have been allowed to face the consequences of their action, parents should take the initiative to reestablish a relationship of trust, compassion and peace in the family circle. Redemptive forces work better in an atmosphere of praise, trust, rewards, mutual respect, and affirmation than in one of harshness, criticism, and condemnation. The more cordial and pleasant parents are with their children, the firmer they can afford to be in setting limits and enforcing consequences, and the less turbulent will be their relationship with them. Redemptive discipline teaches the power of forgiveness, a collateral virtue that could mean the difference between life and death for our children. As children are forgiven of their misdeeds and gain **redemption** into the fellowship and trust of the family, so also must they learn to forgive those who have wronged them.

Children need to learn that there *are* moral absolutes and that all humans are answerable to God. Teaching a child to obey his parents is an essential step in teaching him to obey God. The latter does not happen without the former, for honoring and obeying parents is the first step in honoring and obeying God.

Discipline without love breeds rebellion. Love does not cause pain, but it permits it. Humans and animals learn from pain. It is said that a cat will not sit on a hot stove twice, and neither will it sit on a cold one either, after it has been burned once by a hot one. The disciplining of our children should never be done in anger, frustration, disrespect, or disregard for a child's personhood. In disciplining children, excessive restriction is just as damaging as excessive permissiveness. Either extreme ultimately produces frustration, resentment, and rebellion.

HOW TO TEACH OBEDIENCE

Every God-honoring parent can be OSIE-CER smart. They can develop and implement a "SMART" action plan (see below) for teaching obedience and training their children for self-management. The OSIE-CER method works wherever children are being trained and nurtured into becoming godly offspring. The acronym "SMART" provides a rationale and actionable tool for using the OSIE-CER design to establish a training program to facilitate self-government in children.

- **(S) Set**–Set specific standards, goals, and rules of conduct. As best as possible, use age-appropriate language and illustrations to be sure children understand common family goals and expectations, and code of conduct. Make the rules as few as possible and explain to children the rationale behind each one.

- **(M) Measurable**–Even as children grow physically one millimeter at a time, so also will they grow incrementally in their understanding and ability to obey codes of conduct and rules. Children will always make mistakes. So a parent should set measurable, age-appropriate goals for their children, remembering always that even the sinless Christ grew daily "in wisdom and stature and in favor with God and man." Many parents use a growth chart to track the physical growth of their children. They can also use a growth chart for obedience to acknowledge progress toward desired obedience goals.

- **(A) Attainable**–The bar for success could be set so high that even adults would have difficulty reaching it. If children feel that the standard is set beyond their ability to achieve, they will become frustrated and even rebellious. In setting expectations for obedience, it is better to raise the bar incrementally, rather than setting it so high in the first place that success is impossible. Parents should never place their children in a situation where failure is inevitable or success is impossible.

- **(R) Reinforce**–Positive reinforcement is exponentially more effective in encouraging desired, repeat behaviors, than is negative reinforcement in eradicating undesirable behaviors.

Teaching children to obey works better in an atmosphere of affirmation and commendation than in one of criticism, put downs, and condemnation. Using external motivation (rewards) to reinforce and encourage desired behaviors should only be a start. Intrinsic motivation for obedience is a more effective and long-lasting way of inculcating the virtue of obedience.

- **(T) Time**–It is important that children know that they do not have ten years to begin to be obedient. Although not all children mature developmentally at the same pace, parents can set timed benchmarks to monitor progress toward certain desired outcomes. Some timelines could be set for *now*–"I expect you to remove your book bag from the family room now." While others could be set for longer periods of time–"I would like you to have your room cleaned up by Sunday at 6 PM." Although deadlines can be nerve rattling at times, it seems most people do their most productive work when they know they must meet a specific deadline. If it works for adults, it will work for children.

- **OSIE-CER SMART FAMILY ACTIVITY:** Discuss and document more ways in which you can teach the virtue of obedience to children.

SUMMARY

Obedience and discipline go together. One cannot be attained without the other. Habits of obedience to parents and to God, earn a child great rewards in this life and the next (Exodus 20:12). Habitual obedience or disobedience will affect the child in every area of his or her life.

The Priest Eli failed to discipline his two sons and they all suffered untimely deaths as a consequence (1 Samuel 3:11-14). Mr. and Mrs. Manoah, the parents of Samson, also had the Eli syndrome: children were in control of the household. Samson did not learn obedience and he paid dearly with the loss of his strength, then his eyes and then his life (Judges 13-16). Children are enjoined by God to honor and obey their parents and not the other way around. Ellen White is unabashedly poignant on the importance of proper home discipline:

> There is no greater curse upon households than to allow the youth to have their own way. When parents regard every wish of their children, and indulge in what they know is not for their good, the children soon lose all respect for their parents, all regard for the authority of God or man, and are led captive to the will of Satan. The influence of an ill-regulated family is widespread and disastrous to society. It accumulates in a tide of evil that affects families, communities and governments.[19]

Obedience! Don't allow your child to leave home without it. For, as a wise sage once said, "Character does not reach its best until it is harnessed, controlled, and disciplined." Be "smart" about teaching obedience and developing disciplined, God-fearing children—use God's design for child management—the OSIE-CER method of nurturing children to self-management. Remember, *redemptive* discipline is the most effective method of teaching the virtue of obedience and the discipline of self-management.

4
The Third Virtue
Order

"But everything should be done in a fitting and orderly way."
(I1Corinthians 14:40)

Many years ago, I was on a social studies field trip to Washington, D.C. with a group of students. The night after we arrived in the city, we fed everyone and called an early bed time since everyone must have been tired, we thought. At 10 p.m., I did a room check to ensure that all the young men were present and accounted for–in bed. When I opened the door to one of the boys' room, I was greeted by wall-to-wall clothes on the floor. I asked myself: "How could this have happened after only about 45 minutes in the room?" I don't know if it was by design or default, but the boys had carpeted the floor with their belongings. It was downhill from there, for the rest of the week.

A young mother once told me a story about how she tried her best to teach her three children the virtue of order and keeping the family's living space orderly and clutter free. The children would do well for a while and then slip back into their old habits of messiness. She decided that she would solve the problem by action and not by words. At the end of each day, she would take a broom and sweep everything that was out of place into a pile and throw it all into the trash bin. The next day the children would be frantically looking for their backpack, shoes, sweater and whatever they could not find. After their frantic search they would invariable turn to their mother and ask: "Mommy, have you seen my ...?" to which mom would respond with a question of her own." Where did you leave it?" "I'm certain, I left it right there mommy?" "Well, keep looking honey!"

After going to school for a few days with their lunch in brown bags, books in hand, and no sweater to keep them warm, the children got the message. Soon, enough, they remembered that her message to them was always, "a place for everything and everything in its place." They had learned the value of keeping things in order.

I called up this mother recently. Her children are now young adults. Two of them are married. She reported to me that they keep a neat and orderly home, and that she is very proud of them. As with other virtues, if order is taught and learned when children are young, there is a strong probability they will not depart from it later in life.

It may seem strange to some that a thing as basic as order is one of the virtues that I am advocating that children learn before age seven. But read on. I believe that before the chapter ends, you will understand why. There may also be questions in your mind about the value of order in raising godly offspring. Order is basic to so many things in life—productivity, progress, goal attainment, family happiness, and so much more. Even the mental, physical, social, and spiritual development of a child is calibrated by God to happen in an orderly and sequential way, so that the child can maximize his or her true potential at every stage of development, as he or she increases "in wisdom and stature and in favor with God and man."

Postmodern children are growing up in a mostly chaotic and lawless society. Physical development is a complex process but it happens in an orderly manner. From the time of conception, an embryo develops into a fetus and the fetus develops into a fully formed child, everything happening in an orderly sequence, within a specific time period, for a specific reason.

The word "order" is scary to many parents because they *think* they do not have the time and energy to keep everything orderly. But the fact is, order saves time! As I prepared to write this chapter, I did some informal research to find out what people thought about order and disorder. I talked with dozens of individuals and asked them one simple question: "Which makes you more productive in life, order or disorder?" The answers were overwhelmingly, "order." Out of curiosity I followed up with a second question to some of the respondents: "Why does order make you more productive?" And the answer to that question was invariably, "It saves me time."

Defining Order

I like the *American Heritage Dictionary's* definition of order: "A condition of methodical or prescribed arrangement among component parts, such that proper functioning or appearances is achieved." This definition contains the pivotal concept–proper functioning–of this virtue called "order." Some synonyms of the word "order" are: regularity, symmetry, harmony, tidiness, neatness, systemization, organization, and structure. Without the presence of order, nothing functions properly on earth or in heaven. The starry atmosphere is a masterpiece of order and precision. Untold trillions of stars and galaxies obey the order in which God placed them. Any departure from that order would spell incalculable disaster for the heavens and the earth. Scientists tell us that the galaxy we live in is spinning at an incredible speed of 490,000 miles an hour. But even at this breakneck speed, every heavenly body maintains its orbit in an unending orderly synchrony.

The Importance of Order for a Child

An important lesson for every child to learn very early in life is the lesson of cause and effect–that to every action there is a reaction.

Teaching children the value of order is an effective way of teaching them the lesson of cause and effect.

Children begin to learn by observing everything around them from the day of their birth. Most of what they will learn during their prime time and super-charged development period—ages 1 to 4—will be as a result of what they see, feel, smell, taste, and hear. Like language development, learning about order happens through a complex and almost inexplicable sequence of brain operations. After months of sensing the environment, a child is able to speak words and even do simple tasks of placing objects in the proper order, without the direct help of a parent. An early introduction to, and understanding of, order is the basis of self-discipline and self-management, which were discussed under the virtue of obedience. As I travel around the United States and to other parts of the world meeting and speaking with parents, one concern that is frequently expressed to me, is how messy their children are. This problem invariably goes back to the days of childhood when order was probably not taught, practiced, valued, encouraged, and reinforced. Children *do* live what they learn!

The Genesis of Order

Follow me now, as I establish the biblical rationale for order. The divinely logical sequence of the creation week is a divine lesson on the value and importance of order to God, in the universe and in one's personal life. As you follow, keep in mind this key text about order/structure/sequence: "There is a time for everything and a season for every activity under heaven" (Ecclesiastes 3:1).

"In the beginning, God created the heavens and the earth" (Genesis 1:1). The Bible begins with a declaration of the creative power of God and the establishment of the principle of order. As God began His creative work, He sequenced the things He created during the first week of creation in an orderly pattern. At creation, the earth was chaotic, empty, and without form (Genesis 1:2). In God's first act of creation, He established order out of a chaotic earth and that order has been the hallmark of all of creation in the universe.

Let's take a look at the ordered events of creation week as God created the earth and its occupants in a logical and orderly manner. Because there was darkness over the earth, it was necessary for God to separate it from light. The evening (darkness) He called night and the light He called day (Genesis 1:3). The night/day order has been uninterrupted since creation. Humans, plants and animals depend on that order for so many of the functions of life. The order of evening and morning along with the weekly cycle of seven days was established by God and man has not been able to alter it.

God then established the order of the sky and the land. He separated the expanse above and the sea below. "God called the expanse 'sky' … and the dry ground 'land.' And the gathered waters he called 'seas'" (Genesis 1: 6-9). The order of sky, land, and sea has remained a reliable separation of elements from the day of their creation.

The Creator's next act in the establishment of order was to create vegetation. These could not have been created before light, darkness, sky, and land, for they needed all those elements to survive. Seed-bearing plants would establish the order of propagation for the years to come, an order that has been as reliable as God Himself.

As creation progressed, order was further established as God created the permanent lights in the sky (sun, moon, and stars) that would govern day and night and the seasons of the year (Genesis 1:14-19). With water and the sky in place, God created the creatures of the sea and the birds in the air. These creatures of the sea depend on water to survive and the birds of the air depend on the sky to live. Had God created the fish and the birds before creating their habitat, they would not have survived a day. This is another key point in understanding the value of order.

With vegetation for food in place, God then created the animals, each according to its kind. And, of course, their habitation and food were prepared ahead of their arrival on earth. God looked around at His created works and He saw that everything was good! (Genesis 1:25)

In the final two acts of God's creative work (Genesis 1:26-31; 2:1-3), He created Adam and Eve and the seventh day as a day of rest. God had provided for man's habitat, food, occupation, and after all that, his rest. Rest comes after work, just like day comes after night. That is how God has ordered creation as a lesson for all mankind in all generations. God is, indeed, a God of order and not a God of confusion! (1 Corinthians 14:33). Order is a teacher. Among other things, it teaches the value of organization, precision, efficiency, and time and resource management.

Evidences of Order in Scripture

Order is important for productivity and functionality. It takes infinitely more time to create order out of disorder than it takes to create order in the first place. We already discussed God's penchant for order even as He set out to create the earth. He not only created the earth in an orderly manner, but He also set in motion the entire universe of planets, galaxies and stars in their ordered orbit. Solomon affirmed the Divine Designer's assigning everything a time, place and function when he wrote: "There is a time for everything, and a season for every activity under the heaven" (Ecclesiastes 3:1). Indeed, the order that exists in the universe is a testament to the work of the Divine Designer, for everything has its ordered place, time and function.

As God led the Children of Israel toward their promised home in Canaan, He instructed Moses to organize the people in groups of fifties and hundreds. That was a simple step to promote order and make their management easier. When Jesus lived among men, He also manifested a love for order and structure. On one occasion when the throng of followers needed food to eat, he instructed His disciples to organize the groups in fifties. Undoubtedly, this was to facilitate efficiency of service.

After Jesus rested in the grave following His crucifixion, the scriptures tell us He was resurrected on the third day. When Peter and some of the other disciples arrived at the tomb to verify for themselves that Jesus had risen, they noticed the linen and the grave cloth that wrapped the body of Jesus at His burial: "Then Simon Peter … saw the strips of linen lying there, as well as the burial cloth that had been around Jesus' head. The cloth was folded up by itself, separate from the linen" (John 20:6-7).

Jesus could and should have been in a hurry to get out of that cold and unwelcoming tomb, so much hurry that He could have found a good excuse to not take the time to fold the burial cloth that wrapped His body after His death. But He demonstrated His love for order even at a time when the most important thing about the moment was His resurrection. By that simple act, Jesus reminds us that order is always in order.

Physicians, musicians, pilots, scientists, engineers, chefs, and a host of innumerable other professionals are able to do their work well and reliably because of that one five-letter word—*order*—which is a learned virtue.

So What?

I can almost hear you asking, "Why teach order to a toddler or infant when they cannot even understand what is going on around them?" And the response to that question is simple: "By beholding they are being changed," and what they are to be they are now becoming, as sure as day follows night and spring follows winter. Order is not an in-born, self-emergent behavior. It *is* a learned virtue. Order not only promotes cleanliness, but it also promotes peace, reduces anxiety, saves time, and of course, is a major component of discipline—both personal and corporate. Respect for order is one of those values that is impossible to recall and retrofit children with if it is not taught early in childhood. Just like solving a mathematical problem, if crucial steps are missed or ignored in solving a problem, it is almost impossible to arrive at the correct answer.

Disorder is like a contagious disease. It is never satisfied to contain itself in one space. It invades and consumes everything within its reach. The home is a microcosm of society and if there is disorder in the home, it is certain that there will be disorder in the broader society where children eventually spend much of their time. Disorder overwhelms and often demotivates a person, ultimately causing them to stop trying to make sense of their environment. Disorder is magnetic; it attracts more disorder. It has a mushrooming effect; it grows exponentially over a short period of time.

Disorder Attracts Disorder

In her book, *Home Comforts,* Cheryl Mendelson explains that police across the United States are having great success in fighting crime by applying the "Broken Window Theory (BW). This theory posits that any sign of social or physical neglect in a neighborhood causes people who are predisposed to antisocial conduct to feel more inclined to commit various crimes and misdemeanors. If there is one broken window and it is not fixed quickly, this suggests to malefactors that no one cares or that no one is in charge. By applying the BW theory, police have found that by attending to the first broken window in a neighborhood, they have been able to halt or slow down social deterioration and drastically reduce serious crime rates. The bottom line is that brokenness attracts brokenness.

Disorder and the Broken Window Theory

I believe that the Broken Window Theory has a related lesson in it about order and neatness in the home. Try leaving dirty dishes in a sink at home and see how quickly it attracts more dirty dishes. A messy room will invite more mess and before long the mess will spill over to other areas of one's dwelling space and also to areas of one's personal and professional life. My mother had a favorite saying when I was growing up, "Cleanliness attracts cleanliness and dirt attracts dirt." How true! She was in actuality stating the BW theory and did not know it.

Although an orderly home is a more inviting place than a disorderly place to dwell in, the desire for perfection and orderliness should not be so compulsive that children cannot enjoy their home. Home is a place where children should be allowed to live free of tension and anxieties that will most definitely negatively impact their psychosocial and spiritual expression and development. Everyone in the home—children and adults—should know what their role is in helping to keep the common spaces neat and orderly.

HOW TO TEACH CHILDREN ORDER
Boot Camp 101

The use of the term "boot camp" here is not to suggest rigidity in training children to learn the virtue and value of order. Excessive rigidity will breed rebellion.

However, like boot camp training for the armed forces, boot camp training 101—home style edition—should be experienced by all children. The reality is that children are going to be trained by *someone* about something or even about everything. Even if children are left to themselves, they will not grow up in a neutrality zone where they learn nothing good or bad. The term "boot camp" sounds awfully intimidating and rigid for young children. However, the reality is that either the forces of good or the forces of evil will take over the training of our children. There is no escaping this reality.

God-honoring parents know that if the enemy takes over the

training of their children even within this virtue of orderliness, she or he will ultimately lead them to frustration and ruin. My musician friends tell me that the sooner you expose a child to learning the violin, flute, piano, etc, the easier it is for them to learn, develop and retain the requisite skills for becoming great musicians. I know many parents who have their children attend "music boot camp 101," even over the protests of their little cherubs. I have seen my share of child prodigies and as I engage their parents in discussing their phenomenal skills, a three-part explanation seems to always come through: "Early start, lots of practice, and great sacrifice." May I suggest that it is no different with the seven virtues that each child should develop before the age of seven, and that definitely includes order as one of the pivotal virtues. Orderliness, neatness, and cleanliness share a common ancestry–God.

A Place for Everything and Everything in its Place

A frequent lament I hear from parents is how messy their children are. "How do I get my child to keep his/her room orderly and clean?" is the inevitable question.

Messy rooms do not suddenly appear in the teenage years or in adulthood. Like the huge oak tree that grows from a small seed, so also with order or disorder. Our postmodern world is always in such a mad rush to get there and get it done, to impress and express, that there is barely any time to teach children and consistently reinforce the virtue of order and neatness. Many adults nowadays generally have too much "stuff" in their lives and they pass on that habit of mindless acquisition to their children. That overabundance of everything contributes to messiness in the home and in life.

A place for everything and everything in its place is best learned at home and not at school. If a child has no sense of order at the time of entering first grade, learning its value will become a challenging task for the teacher and the student at every grade level.

The perception of children is different from that of adults. When a child is instructed to clean his room, he may do a great job based upon his perception of "clean." By precept and example, parents must take time to patiently demonstrate to their child what a clean room looks like. It is an exercise in futility when parents ask their children to keep their room clean and orderly, when the parents themselves do not lead by keeping their space orderly and clean. Some of my favorite quips about the value of good examples are applicable here: "A good example has twice the value of good advice." "What can't be done by advice can often be done by example." "Always remember that there are certain people who set their watches by your clock." And the final one, "No one is more confusing than the parent who gives good advice while setting a bad example."

As mentioned before, one of the challenges that parents face in teaching the virtue of order to children is that children, with the help of their parents, acquire too much "stuff." Too much clothes, shoes, toys, gadgets, furniture—just too much of everything. Excess encourages disorder in children for there is always the next one (shoes, toys, etc.), if I cannot find that one. Could it be that most of the money that parents spend on their children today is being wasted, for it is being spent to satisfy wants that create unending clutter?

THE "ABCs" OF TEACHING CHILDREN ORDER

a. Parents, take the lead and welcome your child into a home that has a place for everything and everything is in its place.
b. Parents should lead by example and reinforce children's behavior when they cooperate with the rules for order.
c. Be consistent (but not offensively rigid) in insisting on the established rules for order in the home.
d. Teach children from a young age to share in the responsibility of keeping the home orderly and clean.

e. Teach children to pick up and put away their toys and other belongings when they are through using them.

f. Always remember that your positive, engaging relationship with a child is more important than having everything in its place.

g. Some children will be messy despite your training by precept and example. You have done your part.

h. **FAMILY ACTIVITY:** Discuss and document more ways in which you can teach the virtue of order to children.

SUMMARY

God loves order. He created order and established and celebrated it in His works. The universe is a place where unceasing order guarantees the safe orbit of trillions of moving galaxies, stars, suns, planets, and moons.. Everything in nature has the built-in order gene. That is why humans can reliably predict the coming and going of the seasons, seed time and harvests, sunrise and sunset.

As a human trait, order is not self-emergent. Things left to themselves tend toward randomness and chaos. Even as life cannot emerge from non-life, so also, order cannot emerge from disorder without the direct intervention of people. Toys scattered on a floor, of themselves, will not come together and align themselves in one corner of the room. People who become "clutterers" did not become that way over night. They probably became that way incrementally, and most likely because a leaning toward disorder was not corrected from earlier on in their lives.

Order not only invites more order, it also invites God and His angels to visit the abode of humans, for God Himself is a God of order.

5

The Fourth Virtue Meditation

"But His delight is in the law of the Lord,
And in his law he meditates day and night."
(Psalm 1:2)

Meditation on the Word of God is the beginning of a life of intelligent choices that are based upon eternal principles. Children are only physically young once, but they can be spiritually immature for life. Spiritual or faith maturity begins with leading them to feed on and find delight in the food of spiritual champions—the "pure spiritual milk, so that by it you may grow up in your salvation" (1 Peter 2:2). The pure spiritual milk *is* undeniably the living and dynamic Word of God. There is a host of collateral virtues that fills the life of a person who takes time to meditate on the Word of God. Meditating on God and the things of God is worship at its best!

The lead story for this chapter on mediation as a cardinal virtue is a true story. The man in the story is my father and the story is one that I watched unfold over six decades and counting. My parents are God-honoring Christians. As a farmer, my father not only provided physical food for his family, but he also provided the spiritual food, as the priest of his family of nine children. His most effective method for showing us the true value of spiritual food, was not just in the daily reading of the Bible with us, but more so in his own private devotional times when I often saw him reading the Bible and praying during his alone time with God.

My father took the words of Jesus seriously and literally: "Man does not live on bread alone, but on every word that comes from the mouth of God" (Matthew 4:4). Never would he leave home in the mornings to work on his farm without first gathering his sleepy-eyed children for reading the Word of God. As children we hated it, for we were always robbed of the best part of our early-morning sleep. But today, his children rise up and call him blessed for the Word of God lives in us now, and no one can take that away. As a family, we would have to memorize a scripture for each day of the week. Not a text per week or a text per month. We had to do one for every day. At the end of the week, we would recite all seven texts at family worship time. It is no wonder that my siblings and I are repositories of the hidden treasures of the Word of God in our minds until today.

One evening, after most of my siblings had gone to sleep, I noticed my dad sitting on our verandah with his Bible opened in his lap. He was just staring out into space as if he was star gazing. I thought he was probably worried about something, so I asked him: "Dad, is something bothering you?" He promptly responded and said, "No son. I am just memorizing some texts, and *meditating* on what I have just read." That is where I learned to develop the virtue of meditating on the things of God. Dad's devotion left a lasting impression on me.

Tony Evans, in his book, *The Promise*, writes: "Once you have taken in Scripture, meditation needs to begin. This is the process of thinking something through, musing on it, simmering it the way a good cook simmers a dish until the flavor penetrates all the way through."[20]

Up until the time of his death at 93 years of age in 2015, my dad's favorite book was still the Bible. I have never called or visited him without hearing several texts from his bank of biblical treasures. For dad, meditating on the Word of God was more than a pastime. It is a treasured virtue that transformed his life. My father never made it past the fourth grade in elementary school, but he certainly was a God-inspired teacher by precept and example. "I do not have much schooling," he liked to say, "but I do have a BA degree. That is, the *born again* degree, for that's all that really matters." How true!

Biblical Meditation Defined

The word "meditation" simply means, "a devotional exercise of, or leading to, contemplation." In the context of this book, meditation as a spiritual virtue is discussed from a biblical worldview. When God called young Joshua to lead the Israelites, he gave Him the divine recipe for prosperity and successful living: "Be strong and courageous. Be careful to obey all the law my servant Moses gave you; do not turn from it to the right or to the left that you may be successful wherever you go. Do not let this book of the law depart from your mouth; meditate on it day and night so that you may be careful to do everything written in it. Then you will be prosperous and successful" (Joshua 1:7-8, emphasis mine). These words were not *advice* from God. They were divine *directives* for successful living.

I am sure you will agree with me that this is a loaded text. It has in it God's command to be courageous; His direction in which to walk; His food to eat; His day- and night-time menu; and then His recipe for prosperity and successful living. All of this could be summed up in one phrase: "Meditate upon and obey the Word of God day and night!"

I am yet to meet parents who do not have strong desires for their child to be successful. Success and prosperous living, heaven style, is predicated on meditating, obeying, and living the Word of God. There is no other success that really matters or that will transcend time.

The meditation-as-a-virtue that I write about in this chapter has nothing to do with the meditation that many of the eastern religions practice. The meditation-as-a-virtue that I present to you is a day and night contemplation on the Word of God. Rather than emptying the mind during meditation and allowing it to fill up with humanistic and satanic sentiments, God entreats us to fill it with His Word. This is a winning formula for raising spiritual champions. And there is no better time to develop the virtue of meditating on the Word of God than from the days of the cradle. Meditating on the Word of God is a discipline like learning to play the violin. It must be done over and over until the "notes" (words) of the Scriptures are memorized and become second nature.

Many Competing Voices

Our children are growing up in an age of "truth-ache" and "truth-decay." A tsunami of immorality, relativism, and disregard for the truths of Scripture has reached a destructive magnitude. There are many voices and choices, forces and attractions that are competing for the minds of our children. The ultimate strategist–Satan–is fully aware of what he is attempting to do. If he can get the minds of our children when they are young, he will have them when they are older. Lou Venden, former pastor of my church, once said, "Whatever gets the mind of the man gets the man." And this is also true for our children, for whatever gets the mind of the child gets the child and the man or woman that the child becomes.

Parents cannot be too vigilant in guarding the minds of their children. The best strategy for guarding their minds is to fill them with kingdom values and the things of God: "Whatever is true, whatever is noble, whatever is right, whatever is pure, whatever lovely, whatever is admirable–if anything is excellent or praiseworthy–think about [meditate on] such things" (Philippians 4:8). Children and adults are transformed by what they focus and meditate upon.

The Devil wastes no time in conditioning the minds of our children from birth and imprinting them with his satanic designs. The conditioning of the minds of our children by the devil is a subversive activity. It is a design to eradicate God and the values of His kingdom from their minds, and to educate them in the secular thrills of his doomsday kingdom. The Devil is a master of deception! As our children grow into the teenage years, he tightens his grip on their minds and their conduct. James Dobson, in his book *Children at Risk,* says it powerfully: "Rock concerts subject masses of emotionally needy kids to deafening noises, eerie lights, wild behavior, and godless philosophies. Like an elephant during the night of fire, an adolescent loses his grip on reality" [21]

William Farley writes: "The gospel, rightly understood and modeled, makes Christianity attractive. Effective parents make the gospel so attractive that the world cannot get a foothold in their children's hearts."[22] However, a new culture seems to be colonizing our world these days. The music, movie, and internet industries seem to have conspired to bombard our children with unrelenting doses of deadly Christ-rejecting secularism and anti-God propaganda. And the winner is Satan, the sinister strategist with a diabolical agenda for our children. His number one goal is to capture and destroy his prey (1 Peter 5:8). Parents cannot relax for one moment, but must always be on the offensive and take the first steps to secure every avenue to the minds of their children.

Our children are only safe when Christ is the Master of their minds and character. Neutrality of mind is not an option. Our children are being mastered by God or by the devil and they cannot serve both at the same time. The world does not have a spiritual receiver to receive and interpret the voice of God and respond to the directives of the Holy Spirit. However, those who make Christ their Master and hide His word in their hearts, can tune into the frequency of heaven and listen to God's conversation with them and follow the guidance of the Holy Spirit on their pilgrimage to Canaan.

e-God

Our children are growing up in an amazingly fascinating age of electronic media. There is "e" everything these days: e-mail, e-education, e-banking, e-dating, e-trading; you name it, there is also an "e" version. There is even e-worship. God is the Creator of the laws of physics and science which allow humans to do things that were once thought of as impossible. Man's knowledge has definitely increased. However, God remains the same. He desires a personal relationship with His children, and that is best facilitated when there is two-way communication between Him and them. The words of scripture continue to be God's principal way of sharing His plan of salvation with mankind, and informing us of the plans He has for our future and prosperity (Jeremiah 29:11).

The Bible, as a printed book, has existed for generations and will continue to exist in that form probably until Jesus returns. The introduction of the e-Bible does not change our God from being a personal Savior and Friend into becoming an e-God that is impersonal and just another cyber space occupant. Today, our children have the opportunity to take the Word of God with them in their minds and hands easier than any previous generation. Let us encourage them to never ever leave home without it–the living and transforming printed or e-Word of God. This is truly an opportune time for our children to "text" a scripture to a friend, a sibling, a parent, or anyone.

Meditation, Medication and Memorization

Meditating on the Word of God is spiritual medication for the sin-infected souls of our children. No one says it better than the Psalmist: "How can a young man keep his way pure? By living according to Your word" (Psalm 119:9). It was by the Word of God that Jesus defeated Satan in three grueling temptations in the desert. In each of the temptations, Jesus responded to the Devil by quoting the Word of God: "It is written ..." (Matthew 4:1-4). Our children will only be fortified to defeat the enemy of their souls as they meditate upon, memorize, and hide the Word of God in their hearts. God's Word in the heart is the spiritual immunization that they need to prevent them from developing deadly character flaws. His Word in their heart is their strategic defensive initiative that will surely defeat the incoming darts of the Devil. His Word in the hearts of our children becomes their guiding light: "Your word is a lamp unto my feet and a light for my path" (Psalm 119:105).

David, a man who struggled with character issues, confessed that his only weapon against evil was the Word of God: "I have hidden your word in my heart that I might not sin against you" (Psalm 119:11). Although our children are born with an unfair disadvantage (sinful at birth, Psalm 51:5), the Word of God in their hearts gives them an unfair advantage–it fortifies them to resist temptation. The hiding of God's Word in the hearts of the young does not happen by having multiple Bibles in the home or by a casual reading of the pages of scripture. It happens when deliberate, intentional effort is made to study, meditate upon, and commit to memory, the nuggets of truth that are good for life–even eternal life. God's timeless directive to young Joshua is the same to us and our children today: "meditate on His Word day and night." Meditating on the Word of God must become a love affair for parents and children.

Don't Leave Home Without it

Earlier in the book, I made a statement about the all-knowing God, Who does not give advice; He gives directives. God knew exactly what He was doing and the transformational effect that His Word would have upon the children of the families of Israel. He spoke to these families through their early earthly leader–Moses. The transmission of kingdom values from generation to generation is facilitated by one medium only–the inspired Word of God. So God's instructions to the families of both ancient and spiritual Israel is direct: "These commandments that I give you today are to be upon your hearts. Impress them on your children. Talk about them when you sit and when you walk along the road, when you lie down and when you get up. Tie them as symbols on your hands and bind them on your foreheads. Write them on the door frames of your houses and on your gates" (Deuteronomy 6:6-9).

Our children are drowning in a flood of occult-saturated media enticements. This starves their souls and leaves them malnourished in the precepts of eternal value. The Word of God must become a delightful meal at all times for them. The secular humanists of our postmodern world would rather have our children focus on reading fiction, imbibing entertainment, fun and games, than spending time reading, meditating upon, and memorizing the Word of God. The secularists know that a scripture-infused child of God is a loss to the kingdom of Satan. The parents of today are challenged to offer their children a spiritual diet that is rich in character-building nutrients–a diet, that like David, they will desire and find delight in ingesting and then living according to its principles of righteousness: "I desire to do your will, O my God; your law is within my heart" (Psalm 40:8)

The prophet Amos prophesied that a day is coming when there would be a great famine on earth: "The day is coming, when I will send a famine in the land; not a famine of food or thirst for water, but a famine of hearing the Word of the Lord" (Amos 8:11). Our children can and should prepare for this spiritual famine by feasting on the Word of God day and night.

Soul Security System

The home security business is a multi-billion industry in the United States. Sophisticated wireless motion and heat detectors can alert occupants of the home to any intrusion by uninvited persons or animals. This alert can even be sent to a remote cell phone or computer. There is a soul-security-system that God provides for His children. The Word of God embedded in the heart is the only foolproof security system to alert the soul to danger and defend it from the deadly explosives that Satan will hurl at it. The soul-security-system of Jesus worked perfectly as the Devil tempted Him in the wilderness. Jesus came out the victor and the undisputed champion of the world. Our children will become spiritual champions as the Word of God becomes their trusted soul-security-system.

The Wisdom of the Righteous

Because our children are born spiritually damaged, they need every advantage to grow up and become godly offspring with the ability to defeat the sinister Devil, and become candidates for the Kingdom of God. Our children are no match for the devil who has had 6,000 years of practice at His craft. They need the wisdom of heaven in order to defeat the enemy of their souls. Such wisdom is provided through the ingesting, meditating upon, and obeying the Word of God.

Luke 1:17 speaks of a prophecy that is focused on family reform in the time of the end. Speaking of John as the forerunner of Christ, Luke wrote: "And he will go on before the Lord in the spirit and power of Elijah, to turn the hearts of the fathers to their children, and the disobedient to the wisdom of the righteous—to make ready a people prepared for the Lord." Having read and meditated upon this text, the operative question is: "Where is the wisdom of the righteous found?" Let's allow the Bible to be its own interpreter. Peter answers the question with pinpoint clarity: "And how from infancy, you have known the Holy Scriptures, which are also able to make you wise unto salvation through faith in Christ Jesus" (2 Peter 3:15).

The Bible is poignantly clear—the wisdom that leads to salvation is found in the Holy Scriptures. It is interesting that Peter notes here, that this Scripture was known from the days of *infancy*. The most effective strategy for leading children to meditate upon and memorize Scripture is to introduce them to the Word of God from the days of their infancy–while they are yet very young and the brain is absorbent and malleable!

I was travelling to deliver a sermon recently, and as I travelled I was listening to Charles Swindol (a pastor and Bible teacher) expound on the value of the Word of God. During his sermon, he defined for his listeners what the "Bible" means–using the Bible as an acronym to mean: "**B**asic **I**nstruction **B**efore **L**eaving **E**arth." He couldn't have been more succinct. He couldn't have said it better! The wisdom to navigate the path to Christ is undeniably found in God's Holy Word. And it is a wisdom that must be experienced before leaving earth to dwell with God eternally.

A Personal Story

I grew up in a family where the Word of God was like a treasured delicacy. Consequently, I have raised my children to study, meditate upon, and memorize scripture the same way I was taught. Today, they are young pilgrims on their way to the kingdom, conducting their lives with the wisdom of the righteous, the Word of God, as their trusted guide and positioning system. It is my continued hope and prayer for them and their children, that their lives will not be short-circuited by the Devil, but that they will diligently take time for their daily "grounding" –meditation on the Word of God.

The story I am about to tell you is one that I was privileged to observe as my brother-in-law and his wife raised their sons, Christopher and Michael, right in the midst of an entertainment-crazy world. Their father, as head of the household, assumed his position as priest of the family and set out to read through the entire Bible with his sons. Often, when I visited their home during the evening worship time, I would sit with them and enjoy listening to and meditating upon a portion of Scripture, which always seemed like I "tasted again for the first time."

Week after week, month after month, and year after year Dave read the scriptures to his sons, and the effect has been gratifying. His sons have surely hidden the Word of God in their hearts, and have grown like Jesus did—"increasing in wisdom and stature and in favor with God and man ..." [23]They have lit their pathway with the lamp of God's Word, discovered the "wisdom of the righteous," and found delight in doing the will of God. As of this writing, both 6-foot-plus sons are: young men of character, born-again Christians, obedient to their parents, and focused on their career goals. I can predict, with a great degree of certainty that they will be like Joshua—prosperous because they meditate upon God's Word day and night. It takes intentionality, anticipatory intelligence, and a committed consistency on the part of parents to feed their children the diet of spiritual champions—the Word of God.

There is nothing more important that parents can do for their children on any given day than to feed them daily on the Word of God. It has been said that, "If parents fed their children physical food as scarcely as they fed them spiritual food, their children would die from starvation and they themselves would be arrested for child abuse." Ouch! But isn't that the stark truth? Charging the spiritual batteries of our children is more important than charging our cell phones for daily use. No charge to our cell phones, no communication with anyone. No spiritual charge to the spiritual batteries of our sons and daughters and they will have no spark or ability to fight against the wily foe.

Positive Sin

Telling the truth as it is, is like iodine on a wound—it may hurt a little but it helps a lot. Robert Murray M'Cheyne (1813-43) is painfully truthful in his poignant words about feeding our children in the green pastures of the Word of God. He makes the case for studying and meditating on the Word of God better than anyone else I know:

> If you do not worship God in your family, you are living in positive sin; you may be quite sure you do not care for the souls of your family. If you neglect to spread a meal for your children to eat, would it not be said that you do not care for their bodies? And if you do not lead your children and servants to the green pastures of God's Word, and to seek the living water, how plain is it that you do not care for their souls? Do it regularly, morning and evening. It is more needful than daily food—more needful than your work."[24]

Jesus is right every time and always will be! "Man does not live by bread alone, but on every word that comes from the mouth of God" (Matthew 4:4). The energy-rich Word of God is the diet that nurtures children to faith maturity. Feeding our children a big spiritual meal on our day of worship won't be of much help to them on Tuesday and Wednesday. The filling gets depleted. A full gas tank will become an empty gas tank sooner or later in a moving vehicle, so also is it with feeding our children spiritual food. They must be fed daily; even if their spiritual tank is filled up one day with the Word of God, it will become depleted as the days go by. The Refilling must take place again and again in order to keep them going.

I am told that the popular Harry Potter movies and books have generated revenues of over $800 billion dollars, because people, and especially the young, could not "get enough" of them. What are children left with after gorging themselves on such a diet of poisonous satanic stew? They are left with nothing but a great introduction into the world of the occult and little or no appetite for the living and life-transforming Word of God. The result: the Devil wins and laughs at our children. If parents are too busy to provide spiritual food for their children, they are too busy indeed chasing the things of vanity that will not transcend time.

Jesus taught us to pray by saying, "Lead us not into temptation" (Matthew 6:13). Do we not lead our children into temptation and make them vulnerable to Satan's attacks when we underfeed them on the diet of spiritual champions—the Word of God?

The Devil likes to fight with spiritually malnourished children because he knows they are weak and vulnerable. Contrary to what postmodern philosophers believe and teach, the Devil is real. He is not just a symbol of evil or a figment of our imagination. His strategy to destroy the Word of God within and outside the hearts and minds of people has never worked and never will, but he keeps trying. Believers must keep him forever a loser by imbibing the Word of God.

Streaking Soldiers

No soldier who hopes to win a battle goes into a conflict without his armor. When a streaking soldier goes to battle, he is on a suicide mission. The Devil knows when our children are underfed with the Word of God, and under-armored without. "The truth buckled around their waist ... the breastplate of righteousness in place ... their feet fitted with the readiness that comes from the gospel of peace ... the shield of faith ... the helmet of salvation ... and the sword of the Spirit, which is the Word of God" (Ephesians 6:14-17). Without the full armor of God, which is the Word of God, the spiritual defense of our children is severely compromised and they become vulnerable to attack by the Devil.

Spiritual weakness is a spiritual food-borne disease. No spiritual food in the soul, no spiritual strength and stamina to fight the good fight of faith. A starving soldier that is armor-less is a DOA soldier–dead on arrival. Do we not set up our children for failure (even eternal loss) when we allow them to streak on to the battle field in a spiritually famished state, to fight against spiritual wickedness, principalities and the powers of darkness? Spiritual champions clothe themselves in the full armor of God and feed daily on the pure, uncontaminated, unadulterated, and life-transforming Word of God.

Appropriately, the Psalmist David concludes: "For I delight in your commands because I love them. I lift my hands to your commands, which I love, and I meditate on your decrees" (Psalm 119:47-48).

HOW TO TEACH CHILDREN BIBLICAL MEDITATION

- Make a commitment to personally feast on the Word of God daily.
- Lead by precept and example and invite children into a love affair with the Word of God and the God of the Word.
- Provide Bibles (in age-appropriate translations) for every member of the household.
- Set aside a specific time to lead the family in reading and meditating on the Word of God.
- Devise a plan to read through the entire Bible over a period of time. Don't allow your children to grow up and leave home without having gone through the Word of God at least once.
- Choose a family key text and have the entire family learn it. It will become the password, pin number, and security code for the family through the years. My family's key text that my wife and children know is from Hebrews 11:24: "By faith, Moses when he had grown up, refused to be known as the son of Pharaoh's daughter. He chose to be mistreated

SEVEN BY SEVEN | 65

along with the people of God rather than to enjoy the pleasures of sin for a short time. He regarded disgrace for the sake of Christ, greater value than the treasures of Egypt, because he was looking to his reward."

- Choose a text per week or per month that the entire family will memorize. Repeat the text whenever part or all of the family is together Repetition reinforces memory.

- Select some key passages in scripture for all family members to memorize. For example: The Lord's prayer; Psalms 1, 23,51, and 100; 1 Corinthians 13; and Revelation 14:6-12.

- Teach your child to do private devotions and read the Bible on his or her own.

- Minimize the use of television and other electronic media in the home.

- Use biblical verses that are put to music to make it easy for your child to memorize Scripture.

- Very carefully screen the reading material of your child. What goes in the mind stays in the mind.

- Preview and eliminate most video games from the pastime activities of children.

- Monitor the company your child keeps. "Bad company corrupts good manners" (1 Corinthians 15:33).

- **FAMILY ACTIVITY:** Discuss and document more ways in which you can teach the virtue of meditation to children.

SUMMARY

Nothing or no one says it better than the Bible. The Bible defends itself better than anyone can. No one can deface or destroy it for it is the Word of the living God. The living Word promises a special blessing to us and our children when we give His Word its rightful place in our hearts and minds. God guarantees: Blessed is the man ... whose delight is in the law of the Lord, and in his law he meditates day and night. He is like a tree planted by the streams of water which yields its fruit in due season and whose leaf does not wither. Whatever he does prospers" (Psalm 1:1-3).

I believe it is safe to conclude that all God-honoring parents want their children to "prosper." That is, to experience good prosperity as opposed to false prosperity. The divine formula for good prosperity is simple: delight in and meditate on the Word of God. There is no such thing as a layaway plan for meditating on the Word of God. *Now* is the time to dig, delve, and dive into the Word of God, meditating upon it precept by precept, so that when the spiritual famine comes, the mind will have its rich reserve of spiritual food to sustain it through austere times.

6

The Fifth Virtue
Surrender

"Submit yourselves, then, to God."
(James 4:7)

A life of surrender to God is the beginning of a life of strength, victory, and divinely-approved success. The word *surrender* does not have a positive ring to it. Even when facing difficulty, human beings have an aversion to surrender because it is associated with weakness, failure, and lack of courage. People value being assertive! They like to be in control of their own direction and destiny. They are afraid to give up control of their lives to anyone, lest others take advantage of them.

Some time ago, I read a story about a group of young men who went swimming at a popular beach on a sunny Sunday morning. Everyone was having fun until the mirth and frolicking was interrupted by blood-curdling screams for help. Two brothers had left the company of their friends and swam out to the not-too-distant barrier reef. While attempting to swim back to join their friends, one of them had a seizure. The healthy brother tried his best to rescue his now disabled brother but to no avail. Both brothers were in danger of drowning.

Very soon, a lifeguard came to help and he did something that made the healthy brother cringe. With the side of his palm, he gave the disabled brother a quick chop in the neck. That relaxed him completely, and without resistance the lifeguard was able to rescue the drowning young man. The young man had surrendered involuntarily to the lifeguard and that saved his life. The moral of the story is that *surrender* and not how the lifeguard secured it was what helped save the boy. As we shall see in this chapter, surrender to Christ cannot be a coerced activity. It is only effective when it is voluntary. "I surrender" is one of the shortest sentences that humans can utter, yet it is one of the most difficult for us to say it voluntarily.

The dictionary defines *surrender* as relinquishing "possession or control … to another because of demand or compulsion; to give up in favor of another." However, *surrender* as a spiritual virtue cannot be demanded or commanded. It must be voluntary.

All children are born as rebellious creatures. The seed of rebellion was planted in them from the time of conception. Satan is the progenitor of rebellion and he has passed on his DNA to Adam and all succeeding generations without their their consent. At birth, if rebellion is not arrested and systematically put to death, it will take over the lives of our children like a metastasizing cancer that invades every vital organ of the body, ultimately resulting in sure death. Rebellion is like a habit that becomes stronger and stronger each time it is practiced and reinforced. Contrary to what many people believe, teenage rebellion did not begin at the onset of the teen years. It began from birth.

A prerequisite for surrender is humility. Lucifer certainly did not display any humility when he desired to be like God. Many years ago, I learned a short poem which puts in perspective the value of this virtue as we lead our children to surrender to Christ: "Humility, the sweetest, loveliest flower to ever bloom on Eden's soil. And yet, it was the first to die. It's gone, if it but look upon itself with admiration. And he who dares to claim it his, proves by that very thought that he has it not." As a prerequisite for surrendering to God, Jesus invites us and our children to, "Come learn of me, for I am gentle and humble in heart" (Matthew 11:28b).

Core or Elective

Surrender to Christ is a supernatural and magical process that has no specific timetable or season. Surrender as a virtue is not an elective for the Christian. It is a core virtue and a required grace for all those who desire to change their loyalty from one master to the other—Satan to Christ. But as always in the kingdom of God in heaven and on earth, humans have the power of choice to accept or reject the offer of Christ. Surrender as a spiritual virtue cannot be mandated, coerced, compelled, or commandeered. In a sense, it is like the action of eating or breathing—no one can do it for us. We must do it for ourselves. Therefore, the operative question in this chapter is this: "How do we get children to surrender to Christ so that this tender and pivotal virtue can dwell in them from the days of their youth?" The short answer is through the process of being born-again—conversion.

When you first become a parent, one of your supreme desires for your child is to see him grow and mature normally. It would bother you greatly if your child never learned to crawl, to walk, or to speak, or do the many things that normal children do as they grow. You would do everything within your powers to help facilitate his or her physical, mental, and social development. In the same way, no parent's work is complete until they have led their child to a born-again experience and full surrender to the Lordship of Christ. This is not the job of school teachers, pastors, coaches, or extended family members. It is a work that cannot be outsourced to any educational system, church, or governmental agency, no matter how well-meaning their objectives might be. I once heard a preacher say, "All God-honoring parents are 'cross-eyed.'" That is, they focus intently on leading their children to the only place that really matters–the cross of Christ. Well said indeed!

A Divine Agenda

I know that you have probably read this text over and over again in this book and elsewhere. It *is* the key text of this book and the God-given agenda of parents, and standard of achievement for children, so I'll repeat it here again: "And Jesus grew in wisdom and stature and in favor with God and man" (Luke 2:52). Jesus is the standard for how our children should grow. It is a parent's responsibility to help grow his or her child in all four dimensions in a harmonious way. The four dimensions of growth are like the ingredients for a cake–they must all be mixed together and baked together to produce the desired delicacy. The spiritual development of children is no less important than their mental, physical, or social/emotional development. For that matter, it is more important, because children's spiritual dimension is the vital connection between the human and the divine.

Raising Surrendered Children

Probably nothing is of greater joy to Jesus than for our children to give themselves to Him at the budding of their childhood and in the freshness of their youth. Our children must personally go through a process of conversion from simply being born of the flesh to becoming being born of the Spirit: "Flesh gives birth to flesh, but the Spirit gives birth to spirit" (John 3:6). Parents, no matter how well meaning, cannot make the new birth happen. Conversion and surrender to Christ is a process and not an event. Surrender is a prerequisite of the new birth, for the new birth is a declaration that a child has left the control of one master and surrendered to a new master. In this book, surrender to Christ is the same as the new birth experience and vice versa. William Farley says it convincingly: "New birth normally comes to children through the teaching, example, and relationship that they have with their parents, especially their father. Parents are God's means of grace given to effect the child's conversion." [25]

It is a divine privilege of parents to teach their children to bring their sins and concerns to Jesus and ask for His forgiveness and help. In this way, they can lead their children to experience the virtue of personal surrender to Christ, and to understand the beauty of the principles of heaven. A parent's faith, no matter how sincere and attractive, cannot be a "hand-me-down" faith to their children. There comes a point in the spiritual journey of children when they must make their faith their own and personally accept Christ as *their* Savior.

We already established the fact that children are born with a spiritual congenital heart defect. At birth, they are half alive–physically alive but spiritually dead. They come to us with a rebellious nature, the same nature that caused the first problem in God's perfect universe. They need to be born again. For as a wise sage once said, "If we are only born once we will die twice. But if we are born twice we will only die once." Any loving parents would spend everything they have to help correct a physical heart defect that their child was born with. The health of their children is a top priority for all parents.

My five year old grand niece was recently diagnosed with cervical cancer. Her parents were devastated beyond belief. And rightly so! An MRI showed that there was a growing tumor in their daughter's tiny body. Her physician decided that surgery was the only way to remove the tumor and give this darling child a chance to live.

After she was prepped for surgery, in a typical surgical pause to clarify procedures, the doctors decided to do another MRI to determine the exact location of the malignant mass that was growing inside of her. The church family of her parents, and relatives and friends from around the world had prayed earnestly for God to heal this child before surgery. And He did! The new MRI could not locate the mass and the surgery was cancelled. Praise God for whom all blessings flow! He still answers prayer.

The spiritual health of our children is even more important than their physical health, for physical health will not determine where they spend eternity. The second birth, acceptance of Jesus as their Lord and Savior, is the gateway to eternal life with Him. Hence, the absolute necessity of the new birth to correct the spiritual heart defect that our children are born with. This new-birth experience in children is a process that happens, not so much because of the precept and example of parents, but as a mystical and miraculous doing of the Holy Spirit. Affiliating with a Christian family or a Christian group can help, but does not necessarily lead a child to surrender to God or to experience the new birth. As the old saying goes, "Your child can sleep in the garage for years but that won't make him a car."

The "Eternity" Implant

Once our children are born, Satan stamps their life with an expiration date, and proceeds to waste no time in arresting them for future crimes—holding them captive to a life of rejecting God and following unrighteous living. But although our children are born with a sinful nature that was in essence an eternal death sentence, they were also created to live forever. God guaranteed that in the very beginning when He restored the freedom of choice to humanity. He declared Satan and his host defeated and doomed, and set in motion an irreversible plan to redeem mankind through His Son, whom He would send to die for their restoration and redemption (Genesis 3:15). God confirmed His guarantee of eternal life for His children by declaring in Proverbs 3:11 that, "He has also set eternity in their hearts." This is spiritual genetic engineering at its best. Every child is trade-marked for and by God, with an implant from His own being—eternal life. From the time of their conception, God plants the "eternity seed"—the ability and desire to live forever in heart of every boy and girl. That seed remains alive, but dormant, until it is activated and germinated by the act of surrender and conversion.

That "eternity seed"/DNA of eternal life that God plants in each child's heart, is what some theologians call the divine spark. It is like a pilot light in a gas-burning stove that remains a tiny flicker until it is set ablaze by the turn of a dial. It is the supreme desire of God that all His children will allow His Spirit to activate the eternity seed in their hearts, nurture it with the flammable living water of life, so that, "Our sons in their youth will be like well-nurtured plants, and our daughters will be like pillars carved to adorn a palace" (Psalm 144:12).

The virtue of surrender happens when a child comes to know Christ personally and understands His plan of eternal life for him. Our children are pre-programmed for eternity. Plants are positively phototropic—they respond to light. Similarly, children are positively "Christo-tropic"—they naturally lean toward their Maker, if adults do not prevent them.

Spiritual Birth Certificate

One fifth grader I met recently told me a fascinating story. At the age of 5, she received a heart transplant and she bubbled with joy for her new lease on life. Her mother later told me that her daughter had been born again—physically for a second time.

Every follower of Christ, young or old, needs a spiritual birth certificate. It is their passport to heaven. Jesus was emphatic in answering Nicodemus' question about the requirements for entering the kingdom of God: "I tell you the truth, no one can see the kingdom of God unless he is born again ... Flesh gives birth to flesh, but the Spirit gives birth to spirit" (John 3:3-5). Jesus' answer to Nicodemus establishes the fact that when our children are born they are of flesh only and devoid of His Spirit. It is a God-honoring privilege for parents to have the ability to give birth to children in the flesh, but only the Spirit can give birth in the Spirit. Our children are born spiritually damaged and spiritually depraved. "The wages of sin"—death—is upon them even before the time of their entry into the world. They need a Savior and a new-birth certificate and a new experience of transformation.

The best and most of the resources of the home, church and church school should be expended, without apology, to evangelize children, leading them to a life of surrender and service to Christ. For, until our children are born-again, they are captives of the Devil, who has imprinted them with his evil nature from the time of their conception.

The Age of Accountability

Children are very much like roses, which are some of God's most beautiful creations. A blooming rose must open on its own time schedule. If it is forced open, it will be destroyed, and if it is left too long on the stem in the garden, it will be useless in a floral arrangement. So it is with children: time is everything.

As we discuss the virtue of surrender/conversion, an obvious question to address is: "Are children born saved or lost?" Even before children make a choice to sin, they are sinners, for they are born with the sin germ in them (Psalm 51:5). Every child needs an extreme makeover, spiritual edition. Before children can reason enough to know the difference between right and wrong, parents are responsible for their moral welfare and bear the responsibility for them before God.

In education, readiness is a key concept in the teaching and learning process. The spiritual readiness of our children cannot be calendared, or preprogrammed. Each child matures physically, mentally, socially, and spiritually at a different pace, so the age of accountability to God will be different for each child. An interesting story emerges from numbers 20:11-12. Because of his disobedience, God denied Moses from entering the Promised Land. Instead He chose Joshua to lead the people. Having heard of his fate, Moses said to the people: "The little ones that you said would be taken captive, the children *who do not yet know good from bad*–they will enter the land." (emphasis mine). God clearly allowed the children who did not know right from wrong to enter the Promised Land. Could it be that this is God's way of relating to children according to their level of maturity and age of accountability? My own experience in working with thousands of children over the past thirty years is that very young children can become Christians commensurate to their years. I have witnessed scores of them who exhibit faith in Christ and who live by the values of His kingdom.

Parents have the right to say "yes" or "no" to demands of their children that they feel will not be for their best good. But there is one request that a child makes that a parent should never answer by saying, "no," "not now," or "I don't think you understand what you are asking for." That request is the one to become a Christian and surrender to Christ as Lord and Master. The most satisfying and eternally significant request that a parent will ever hear from their child is: "Can I be baptized?" I can tell you many stories of parents who have said "no" to that question from their child, and that was the last time that their child expressed any interest in spiritual things. Only God knows when a child is ready to surrender to Him. The biggest and most important decision a child will make in his life on earth is the one to surrender to Christ. All of heaven rejoices over that.

There seems to be no fixed chronological time that determines when the age of innocence ends and when the age of accountability begins. We do know that God calls upon children to remember Him in the days of their youth (Ecclesiastes 12:1) and that when Jesus was on earth, He would constantly draw the children to himself and use them as commercials for demonstrating what the kingdom of heaven is like. The virtue of surrender/conversion is not self-emergent. It will not happen naturally just because it is a latent virtue waiting to manifest itself in children. It must be introduced, nurtured, triggered, encouraged, acknowledged, and celebrated when it happens. The Bible says there is great rejoicing in heaven when one sinner changes sides and surrenders to Christ as Master and Lord (Luke 15:3-7). The greatest accomplishment of any family is to experience the new birth of their child.

Writing in *AWSNA Journal*, David Mitchell labels the first seven years of infancy as the initiation years. He writes: "Apparently helpless in her mother's arms, the infant seems incapable of learning. In fact, the baby is at the most absorptive stage and totally open to external influences. Imitation is the special talent that characterizes the period of up to age six or seven.[26]

Surrender/conversion is a learned virtue that begins at birth and, over time, becomes an acquired grace-of-choice that defines the new relationship of mutual love between God and His children.

A Fruit Analogy

As an avid gardener, I have learned a few lessons from nature that have special meaning for the spiritual life of believers. Many years ago, I planted an apple tree that would produce my favorite Gala apples yearly. It did not take me long to realize that after the blossoms are out in the spring, the fruits would develop at a different rate and to different sizes. Each apple would also ripen on its own schedule. As a result of that, I would have apples to eat over a three-month period instead of all of them ripening for harvest on the same day.

I have also noticed that my tomatoes and bell peppers, although given the same growing conditions and bearing on the same vine, do not all mature on the same day. Young fruits and vegetables are perfect at every stage of their development. The mature ones can *only* come from the younger and immature ones. Faith maturity is a divinely scheduled process and over time, the spiritually-mature children develop from the immature little ones.

And one more thing about my fruits, they must be reaped at the right time, otherwise, the birds will get them or they will fall from the tree and rot. It is for me as the gardener to know when it is prime time to reap. For in order to reap mature and delicious fruits and vegetables, timing is everything. So also is it with children. Timing is crucial as we develop and prepare them for making that most important decision of their lives—their commitment to Christ as their Savior.

Although different children in the same family may be given the same growing conditions and the same exposure to the claims of Christ on their life, they will "ripen" or come to spiritual maturity at a different pace and consequently in their own time. The most special, most important, and most rewarding task of parents is to invite their children to surrender to Christ and to facilitate that process when the time is right. Then it will be time for celebration extraordinaire—heaven's style!

Age Is of No Consequence

It is always a puzzling question about the age at which a child is mature enough to surrender to Christ and become a Christian by choice. As established earlier in the chapter, faith maturity is not a set chronological event, for each child matures at a different pace, just like in learning to crawl, walk, talk etc., children will develop on a different time schedule. So it is in spiritual maturity. It is a process, and sometimes, oh so imperceptible!

An eminent religious leader was asked: "How old should a child be before there is reasonable hope of being a Christian?" Her answer was, "Age has nothing to do with it,.....Love to Jesus, trust, repose, confidence, are all qualities that agree with the child's nature. As soon as a child can love and trust his mother, then can he love and trust Jesus as the Friend of his mother. Jesus will be his Friend, loved and honored."[27]

The age at which a child learns to love and trust his mother will vary for every child. But that, according to the above statement, is a good benchmark for determining the readiness of a child to surrender to Christ and become a Christian. This position is clearly not an argument in favor of infant baptism. Only when children have developed the capacity to love and trust their parents are they ready to love and trust their Savior.

According to Hebrew tradition, children were weaned from their mothers by age three. That means Samuel was placed in the temple to serve God and learn the priesthood from a very tender age. Children often have more learning capability than some adults credit them with.

LCM–Do the Math

Early in their educational experience, children learn an important mathematics concept that is basic to a good understanding of computation. They learn to compute the "Least Common Multiple" (LCM) of a given set of numbers. As children mature like Jesus did, "in wisdom and stature and in favor with God and man,"[28] they must also deal with a spiritual LCM, for Lord, Career and Mate. It is the duty of parents to lead their children to make the first and most important decision of their lives: "Who will be their Lord (L)?" Answering this questioning correctly will result in the surrender of their life to God and not to the Devil. The winner must be God!

The next important question that children should be led to ponder is: "Why were they born, and hence, what career (C) they will pursue to fulfill that purpose?" God has a special place on earth for every child. He gifts each one of them with talents and abilities that should be developed to serve humanity and glorify Him. Way back in the beginning, in the Garden of Eden, God gave man his work before He gave him a mate (Genesis 2:15-17). The elementary, high school and college years of a child should be used to first answer the question about who is their Lord, and second about the purpose of their life as they pursue the preparation for service through their career.

The final question in the spiritual LCM is: "Who will be my mate (M)?" Every normal child grows up with the God-given ability to romantically love someone of the opposite sex. That is a God-designed, transcendent principle of love that He instituted right there in the Garden of Eden. Children are not mature enough to love a mate until they have developed a love relationship with their Maker and have prepared their life to serve Him and their chosen mate.

God is very much interested in the LCM of His children. When a child's world view is informed by God's Word, it will make an eternal difference on how that child answers each of the spiritual LCM questions. One of the great joys and rewards of God-honoring parenting is not just to facilitate the answering of these questions, but to actually see their children's lives unfold in a God-glorifying way as they surrender to the lordship of their Maker and Savior.

"I Am Very Pleased"

The loveliest, sweetest words that will ever fall on the ears of parents and their children are the very words that God the Father spoke of His Son at His baptism, after He voluntarily surrendered to the authority of God, His Father: "This is my Son, whom I love, with him I am well pleased" (Matthew 3:17). It is the hope of every God-honoring parent to hear words of approval from God, affirming them for the work they have done in raising godly offspring for Him. Such words, as the Father spoke of His Son, Jesus, to a parent and to a child, are worth more than all the wealth of the world combined. When God is pleased with us and with our children, it means that we have found favor in His eyes and fulfilled the divine objective for which He brought us into the world.

"Transforming Children into Spiritual Champions"

George Barna has done a great deal of research on children and youth. In one of his studies cited in his book, *Transforming Children into Spiritual Champions*, he notes: "The probability of someone embracing Jesus as his or her Savior [is] thirty percent for those between the ages of five and twelve; four percent for those in the thirteen to eighteen age range, and six percent for those nineteen and older. In other words, if children do not embrace Jesus Christ as their Savior before they reach their teenage years, the chance of their doing so at all is slim."[29]

The transformation of our children into spiritual champions must happen sooner than later. For, as the research indicates, it becomes exponentially harder as children grow older. A child may not choose to surrender to Christ before age seven, but at that age he or she is in the prime time for surrendering to one of two masters— Christ or Satan. If the foundation for knowing, loving, and serving Christ has been laid by age seven, it increases the probability of the child becoming and remaining a born-again Christian.

Our children are on the "on-ramp" to Jesus. Just as it is on entering a freeway from an on-ramp, if they back up, there will be danger, damage, and possibly destruction. Satan is gleefully awaiting them to do just that. The only way for them to move in safety is to move forward toward Christ. Parents are tasked with that special privilege of helping to move their children forward in the right direction—toward becoming spiritual champions.

HOW DO WE TEACH CHILDREN THE VIRTUE OF SURRENDER?

- First, surrender self to God and by precept and example live a life of joy and love for God and demonstrate joy in serving Him.
- Consistently model a life of surrender to God before your children.
- Pray with and for your child even before they can verbalize and fully understand the objective of prayer and worship.
- Use age-appropriate language to tell your child about God's love for her or him.
- Focus the family on spiritual things. Allow no gaps between the profession of your faith and the practice of its principles.
- As children mature, explain the importance of surrender to Christ, conversion, and the need to be born-again.
- Invite your child often to give his or her heart to Jesus.
- Engage your child in serving Jesus in and out of the home.
- Say "yes" to your child's first initiative to surrender to Christ.
- Celebrate in a tangible way your child's decision to become a born-again Christian.
- Help your child to follow through with his or her conviction and decision and arrange for baptism by immersion.
- **FAMILY ACTIVITY:** Discuss and document more ways in which you can teach the virtue of surrender to children.

SUMMARY

"It is easier to raise a Christian than to convert one." Teaching children the virtue of surrender should begin at an early age. Parents should help and not hinder children as they grow into faith maturity when they will make a conscious choice to make Christ their Lord and Master. Home evangelism is the number one task of God-honoring parents. Gospel-powered parenting keeps both eyes on eternity, for no other goal will bring satisfaction to God or to humans. No amount of success in a parent's or child's life will compensate for the loss of a soul from the kingdom of God.

The world regards surrender and submission as weak virtues, but where the Kingdom of Heaven is concerned, there is no salvation without them. Children should be intentionally invited, by their parents, to surrender their lives to Christ and submit to His authority. As they exhibit understanding and readiness they should be encouraged to have a born-again experience. The prime time for children to surrender to Christ is during the "days of their youth" for if they make God first in their lives, and seek to live according to the values of His kingdom, He will give them everything else that they need (Matthew 6:33).

There is only one kind of divinely-approved success that will transcend time and last throughout eternity—the success that comes to a child of God when he or she finds delight in meditating on His Word day and night, and in walking in its precepts without wavering (Joshua 1:7-8).

7

The Sixth Virtue
Generosity

"A generous man will prosper;
He who refreshes others will himself be refreshed."
(Proverbs 11:25)

Living a life of generosity is a pathway to the hearts of others and a privileged place in the sanctuary of the heart of God. For both man and God, and even animals love a kind and generous person.

One of the primary goals of parenting must be to teach children how to develop a heart of caring and sharing. When I was growing up, the popular legend about Androcles and the Lion was often told to us children. It is a story about generosity and kindness. Although it is *only* a parable, it has valuable lessons worth pondering. It is worth hearing again as we consider the importance of the sixth virtue to teach our children by age seven.

Here is the *Reader's Digest* version of the story. In Rome, there was once a poor slave whose name was Androcles. His master was a cruel man and so unkind to him that at last Androcles ran away. He hid himself in the wild for many days but there was no food to be found. He grew so sick and weak, he thought he was going to die. One day he crept into a cave and lay down and soon he was fast asleep.

After a while, a great noise woke him up. A lion had come into the cave and was roaring loudly. Androcles was very much afraid that the lion would kill him. Soon, however, he saw that the lion was neither hungry nor angry, but that he limped as though his foot hurt him. Androcles grew bold and took hold of the lion's lame paw to see what the problem was. The lion stood quite still and rubbed his head against Androcles' shoulder. It seemed to be saying, "I know that you will help me."

As Androcles examined the lion's paw, he saw that there was a long, sharp thorn embedded in it. It must have hurt the lion so much. Androcles took hold of the thorn and gave it a strong, quick pull and out it came. The lion was full of joy and jumped like a happy dog, and licked the hands and feet of his new-found friend. After this, Androcles and the lion lay down together and slept side by side. For a long time, the lion brought food to Androcles daily and the two became such good friends that he found his life to be a very happy one.

One day, while some soldiers were passing through the woods, they found Androcles and took him back to Rome. It was the law at that time that any slave who ran away from his master should be made to fight a hungry lion. So a fierce lion was shut up for a while without food, and a time was set for the fight. Thousands of people gathered to see the sport. The door opened and poor Androcles was brought in. He was paralyzed with fear as the hungry lion roared and moved toward him.

As the lion jumped at him, Androcles gave a great shout of gladness, for it was the same lion that had been his friend in the cave. Androcles put his arms around the lion's neck while the lion licked his feet tenderly. The people were filled with wonder. When questioned about how he did it, Androcles told them that he and the very same lion had lived together in the cave for a long time. He told them about how he saved the lion's life by one simple act of kindness and how the lion had fed and protected him in return. The people shouted to the officials: "Let the man go free, and let the lion also go free. Give both of them their liberty." Generosity is indeed its own reward!

Born to Serve Self

Now, allow me to share three of my favorite quotes on selfishness: (a) "A person who is self-centered is off-centered;" (b) "The man who lives only for himself, runs a very small business;" (c) "Master selfishness or it will master you."

Even from very early in life, humans tend to gather and hoard more things than they really need. In an increasingly self-centered world, selfishness and greed parade themselves as self-preservation and the right of the individual to look out for No. 1–self. Selfishness is not just a learned behavior. It is sadly an inherent vice that is asleep in the heart at birth, but sooner or later wakes up to involuntarily take control of one's life. All children are pre-programmed to be selfish and they begin to show it from the day of their birth.

My years of work in churches and schools with young children from kindergarten to university, have exposed me to the cancer of selfishness that wraps itself around the aorta and heart of even the very young. You don't have to be around infants and toddlers for very long before you hear expressions such as: "That's mine; I want that; Leave me alone; No, I don't want to …!" That is the voice of *self* getting ready to serve self unapologetically.

It seems that self-preservation emerges in children even before they are born. Exodus 25:19-26 records the story of Rebekah and Isaac as they prepared to become parents for the first time. Rebekah was pregnant with twins–Esau and Jacob. While they were yet in the womb, a rivalry broke out between them. So the Lord told her: "Two nations are in your womb, and two peoples from within you will be separated; one people will be stronger than the other, and the older will serve the younger" (Exodus 25:23).

Esau was the first of the twins to be born, and as he came out of the womb, his heel was grabbed by his brother Jacob. That was the start of a life of selfishness and dishonesty by Jacob. Selfishness is the seed of many other vices: dishonesty, duplicity, untruthfulness, deception, cheating, and unfairness. Selfishness will do whatever it takes to protect and serve self, even at the expense of hurting others in the process. Selfishness begins as a small seed in the human heart, but as it is fed by self-serving actions, it grows and overtakes the spiritual, mental, physical, and emotional dimensions of people. Small things *can* make a big difference.

Generation Me

Jean Twenge, in her book, *Generation Me,* writes: "This is a generation [that is] unapologetically focused on the individual, a true Generation Me."[30] She further posits that the current generation bought into the premise of Whitney Houston's 1985 No. 1 hit song: that "The Greatest Love of All," was loving one's self. She relates the story of a twenty-five year-old man who had experienced some rough spots in his life. As a result, he came up with a new motto: "Do what's best for me. I have to make me happy; I have to do what's best for me in every situation."

The Generation Me generation regards self, first as a right and not a choice. Selfishness in the heart kills love for others and is an enemy of kindness, compassion, empathy, and generosity. It refuses to, or reluctantly shares anything that will deprive self of taking care of self first. Narcissists are people who display an inordinate love or admiration for themselves. Our children do not start out in life with a conscious decision to be narcissists, but selfishness is like a metastasizing disease that begins small and ultimately infects and affects everything around it. It changes the attitude so that, more and more, taking care of self becomes the passion of one's life. Twenge further contends that: "Narcissism is one of the few personality traits that most psychologists agree is completely negative. Narcissists are overly focused on themselves and lack empathy for others, which means they cannot see another person's perspective. Unlike those merely high in self-esteem, narcissists admit that they don't feel close to other people."[31]

No Man is an Island

When I sang in the choir during my high school years, I learned a beautiful song, the words of which have lingered with me over these many decades: "No man is an island, no man stands alone; each man's joy is joy to me, each man's grief is my own; We need one another, so I will defend, each man as my brother, each man as my friend."

Humans are interdependent creatures. No person can exist without dependence on someone or something else. It is our interdependence that builds engaging and life-refreshing relationships that find their greatest joy in giving and not in receiving. Someone has aptly said, "If it is too much to give, it is also too much to receive." Unselfishness wins over selfishness any day. From very early in their lives, children must be taught the virtue of generosity—thoughtfulness, kindness, compassion, empathy, and sharing, for it is only as they give these graces to others that they will also receive them in return. Why should our children be raised to expect from others what they do not give to others?

Many years ago I was conducting a career workshop for high school seniors. As I interviewed the students to learn about their interests and career goals, I was struck by the answer of one of the students. When I asked, "What are your interests and career goals?" He shocked me with his quick, crisp, and apparently well-thought-out answer: "I want to be independently wealthy by the time I am

30." So I asked him how was he going to achieve that? To that question he also had a strategic design of how he was going to amass his wealth. He had no place in his plan for being kind and generous to others, let alone to God. So I asked him to explain to me, "How does one become 'independently' wealthy?" He stumbled his way through some faint ideas of what *independent* meant to him. After I had shared with him that humans are all interdependent, with each other and even with nature, he seemed to have had an *aha* moment.

I questioned him further about how he planned to give back to society and he promptly responded that after he had amassed his wealth, he would consider being charitable. Little did he know that generosity—kindness, sharing, empathy, compassion, and giving—develops like a tomato plant: you don't get the mature fruits without going through the early stages of development from seed to seedling, to blossom, to young tomatoes and then to mature tomatoes.

Generosity is most productive when it is cultivated in the life from the days of youth. Becoming "independently" wealthy (although that is a misnomer) does not happen by receiving and hoarding. Generosity brings great joy when it happens right alongside with unselfishly sharing with others what the *Theophilanthropist* God has given to us. The answer to the heart's insatiable desire to find joy in life *is* generosity, kindness, and love for God and for one another. And this is a life-saving, joy-producing lesson and virtue that children should learn from early.

The Rich Young Ruler's hoarding, selfishness, and independently wealthy status did not impress Jesus. When this young ruler was asked to show kindness and empathy to the poor he went away sorrowful (Luke 18:18-26). He was indeed empty on full! Kindness to the less fortunate is kindness to God. Generosity is not a dispensary whose sole function is to just give. It is a storehouse for our treasures in heaven. Jesus taught that it is by being generous and kind that we lay up treasures in heaven.

Theo-generosity

In the Greek language, the word *Theos* means God. So *theo-generosity* means the generosity of the Divine. Generosity is defined as "liberality in giving or willingness to give." Generosity *is* the thermometer of love and God is its embodiment. The Bible enjoins children and adults to, "Be devoted to one another in brotherly love. Honor one another above yourselves" (Romans 12:10). Love is the greatest principle in life. It is the only virtue that the Bible says *is* God: "God is love" (1 John 4:16). Someone has said, "You can give without loving, but you cannot love without giving."

When it comes to giving, God stops at nothing! One of my favorite quips on generosity is: "The world is composed of the givers and the takers. The takers may eat better, but the givers sleep better." Probably the greatest joy that could come to anyone in life is the joy of giving. God is a giver. In the beginning, He spent a week creating the heavens and the earth and at the end of it all, He did the very thing that is "so God:" He gave it all away to Adam and Eve. God's act of giving it all away to the First Couple is the essence of *theo-generosity*–God-kindness, compassion and mercy. The Bible is densely punctuated with God's acts of generosity, compassion, mercy, and kindness to humanity throughout all generations. He has modeled for children and adults the kind of willingness to share that He knows will build better human relationships as we provide mutual support for one another.

God's greatest demonstration of *theo-generosity*, however, is in the love that He displayed by giving His life as a ransom for His children. *"Greater love has no man than this..." (John 15:13).* God does His most effective work when He is leading and training by example. God's gift of His Son to the world should compel every believer to develop the virtue of generosity. For no one out-gives God–never has, never will! Even as He was unselfish enough to give His life for all of mankind, so also must we teach our children by precept and example, the beauty of possessing and demonstrating this pivotal virtue of generosity, compassion, empathy, and kindness.

Generosity is not a virtue that can be placed on the layaway plan—with the hope of either developing it later or suddenly incorporating it into one's attitude and way of living at some unspecified time in the future. It is a virtue that must be cultivated from the earliest days of life, for if selfishness is allowed to take root in a child's life, its tentacles reach out and negatively impact the way that child thinks, feels, and acts. Habits, good or bad, become ropes and then chains that are very difficult to break.

Living is Giving

It has been said that, "The best part of living is giving." The sooner our children learn this life-changing truth the sooner they will shift the focus of their attention from "what's in it for me," to "what's in it for others." God, in His multiple displays of *theogenerosity*, demonstrated that other-centeredness is a more blessed thing than self-centeredness: "…Remembering the words the Lord Jesus himself said, 'It is more blessed to give than to receive'" (Acts 20:35).

The renowned song writer, F. E. Belden, penned a song in 1899 that speaks to the theology and beauty of generosity, sharing, kindness, and giving. It says, in part:

> Give! Said the golden sun, up rose the mist;
> Safe in the silver clouds, cradled and kissed.
> Give! Said the thirsty earth, down came the shower;
> Give! Said the raindrops bright, up sprang the flower.
> Living is giving, giving is living;
> All things would die if only receiving.

Generosity, Kindness, Sharing, Giving ... Why?

We already established that it is a law of life that nothing exists of itself or by itself and that "living is giving and giving is living." But the question still lingers: "Why should we teach our children the virtue of generosity?" I could answer with one simple Bible verse: "A generous man will prosper; he who refreshes others will himself be refreshed" (Proverbs 11:25). As succinct as this text is, there is more to this question of why children should be taught the virtue of generosity?

My friend and fellow Rotarian, Manzoor Massey, likes to say, "Kindness is the rent we pay for the free blessings that we received from the great Giver." Therein lies the ultimate objective for developing a generous heart–sharing our lives and possessions with God, the giver of all good gifts. If children do not learn to share what they have with others, neither will they desire to share what they have with God. Sharing with one another rids the heart of selfishness and greed, and prepares the heart for giving of its best to God and receiving from Him in return for more than we could ask or imagine.

The Generosity of a Child–a True Heart Virtue

Few stories in the Bible hold more truth about the virtue of generosity and how the Lord blesses both those who possess it and what they share with others, than the story of the boy who shared his lunch with Jesus and ultimately with thousands. Matthew 14:13-21 records the story of the young boy who followed the crowd to listen to Jesus. This probably was not his first outing with Jesus. No doubt, he was not only learning the words of Jesus about kingdom values, but more importantly, he must have been observing the compassion, mercy, kindness, and generosity of Jesus as He ministered to the needs of the people.

As soon as this lad learned that there was a need for feeding hungry people, he must have desired to emulate this "Wonder Man" Jesus, who was doing so much for the people. His tender heart must have been moved with compassion and his kindness must have led him to willingly share his prized possession—his five loaves of bread and two fish. Jesus took his lunch and blessed it. (Note that Jesus ordered the people to sit down on the grass, probably to create some sense of order). Then the disciples shared the "blessed food" with the thousands of hungry people. They had baskets of leftovers, after everyone had eaten likely to their heart's content. I could only imagine the joy the lad must have felt when he saw that it was his small lunch that was used in this miracle to feed thousands.

The story of the lad and his five loaves and two fish can and should teach our children some valuable lessons about generosity: (1) Nothing is too small or too precious to give to God; (2) When children give what they have, God will multiply it and use it to bless others; (3) What they have is not theirs until they are willing to share it with God and others; (4) Compassion, generosity, kindness, sharing flow out of a heart of love for God and for His children; (5) They should give *not* to get, but they should get *to* give; (6) What they get in return for what they compassionately give, is not so much material blessings, but priceless joy; (7) As in the story of Androcles and the Lion, God does not always give us what we may want in return for what we give. He gives us what we need.

As children develop and practice the virtue of generosity, compassion, mercy, kindness, and giving throughout their lives, it will become easier for them to return not only their lives to God, but also to return to Him a faithful tithe and offering (Malachi 3:8) in gratitude for His blessings to them. Generosity is the antidote for selfishness, greed, and narcissism. If our children refuse to share with their fellow human beings, it is almost a certainty that they will also refuse to share with God. Generosity to man or to God is an act of thanksgiving—thankfulness that "No man is an island, no man stands alone …" and so we need each other, and that God, in His great love, compassion, and mercy is the giver of all good gifts to us.

Generosity in Working Clothes

Not too long ago, a good news/sad news item was reported on the evening news. Eight-year-old Rachael Beckwith had set out to raise three hundred dollars by her ninth birthday to bring clean water to people in poor countries. Rachael was about eighty dollars short of her goal when a horrific traffic accident took her life. As the news of her unselfishness emerged after the tragedy, thousands of people from around the world pitched in to help raise the required funds for the clean water project.

Within days of her death, over two hundred thousand dollars were contributed to her cause. Now because of the unselfishness and generosity of one little girl, thousands of people will benefit from having clean drinking water in their villages. Rachael not only cherished a desire to do some good during her lifetime, but she put her generous heart in "working clothes" and accomplished more in her death than she dreamed she could possibly accomplish in her lifetime. May her soul rest in peace for her reward is sure in God's kingdom. "God loves a cheerful giver" (2 Corinthians 9:7).

HOW TO TEACH GENEROSITY

- Be a kind, generous person yourself. The power of example is the greatest and the most enduring influence on children
- The development of any virtue happens better in an atmosphere of praise, appreciation, and positive reinforcement, than in one of criticism, condemnation and punishment.
- Help your children to see the big picture—that they are rich compared to much of the world.
- Provide opportunities for children to share from their days of infancy and acknowledge and reinforce desired behaviors each time they are displayed.

- Use age-appropriate language to explain the value of sharing to children. They have the ability to understand more than we think they can.
- Be *consistent* in reinforcing acts of kindness and sharing and also in actively discouraging acts of selfishness.
- Get involved in community charities and engage your child in sharing what they have.
- During the holiday seasons, engage your children in the act of giving rather than in the expectation of receiving.
- Teach children that true giving is not a matter of parting with what they do not need, but actually giving something they do need.
- Teach them that true generosity and giving involves sacrifice and self-denial.
- Lead your children to adopt a project that will involve them sharing in a way that will make a difference in the lives of less fortunate people.
- Engage your child in a local or overseas mission trip to serve in an area of need.
- Lead by example by giving a faithful tithe and offering to your local church.
- Teach your children the principles of tithing and help them calculate their weekly/monthly contributions.
- Develop and practice a vocabulary of affirmation in teaching and reinforcing any or all of the virtues: "great job, fantastic, outstanding, great, lovely," etc.
- **FAMILY ACTIVITY:** Discuss and document more ways in which you can teach the virtue of generosity to children

SUMMARY

All humans are born with a selfish nature and a strong desire to receive rather than to give. At birth, children are unaware of their own selfish nature. If left unchecked, that selfishness will corrode their hearts and ostracize them from the very people with whom they are interdependent for survival.

Generosity of spirit and heart is the antidote for selfishness. The Bible promises, with certainty, that those who give to others will be blessed in return: "Cast your bread upon the waters for after many days you will find it again (Proverbs 11:1). Being generous and kind is like having a savings account that gives interest (dividends) upon that which is deposited. A selfish person knows no joy, but selfless and generous persons know the true joy that comes from a life of living and giving.

For children as well as for adults, if something–a good deed, kind words, loving favor–is too much to give, it is also too much to receive. The greatest act of generosity is giving with no expectation of anything in return. That is the essence and fulfillment of agape love–*theogenerosity* at its best. It is a love that gives and gives and gives!

8

The Seventh Virtue
Trust

"Trust in the Lord forever, for the Lord,
the Lord, is the Rock eternal."
(Isaiah 26:4)

Trust in God is the beginning of eternal life for the believer. Trust is the basis of all human relationships between man and God and between humans. Trust, like eggs, must be handled with care, for trust once broken, like eggs once broken, is nearly impossible to be repaired. Trust is a virtue that works best when it is a two-way interpersonal interaction. Humans are relational by nature and cherish a deep desire to have positive interpersonal relationships with the people in their lives. In raising children, trust is not an elective virtue. It is one of those core graces that all who will surrender to Christ and live peacefully with his fellowman must develop and display.

Many years ago, I watched the unfolding of a nail-biting news story on the evening news. It was all captured on one of those ubiquitous cell phone cameras and then beamed on television screens during the evening news. A three-story apartment complex caught fire with an unknown number of residents inside. Before the firemen arrived, several brave, local residents rallied to the cry for help and rescued those residents they could find in the burning building. The building was near the point of collapse when frantic onlookers spotted a screaming little boy waving from a window in a smoke-filled room. With fire all around, he was trapped in the room with no way of escape. The room was three floors up and it was too late for even the bravest of rescuers to enter the flaming building.

The men on the ground yelled to the 10- year-old boy, "Jump, jump!" By his own confession, the little boy thought for a moment, "One way or the other I am going to die so I'd better make a go for it." The men on the ground quickly formed a circle that would function as a safety net and shouted to the boy once more, "Jump! Now!" The boy trusted in their confident command, and quickly jumped (from about thirty feet up) into the safe arms of the men below. There were sighs of relief and shouts of joy. Johnny had an elevated heart rate when he landed, but he was unhurt.

By the time the firemen arrived, the building was engulfed in flames. They quickly put out the fire. When the commotion settled, one of the firemen asked Johnny, "What made you jump from so high up?" His reply: "I trusted the men." Trust is a virtue that can only be acquired through cultivation as people learn to be authentic, reliable, credible, and transparent.

Trust: The Multivitamin of Virtues

A "vitamin is any of various fat-soluble or water-soluble organic substances essential in minute amounts for normal growth and activity of the body." In a sense, trust is the multivitamin of the virtues. It is essential for the development and practice of all the other virtues. In the dietary world, organic vitamins are labeled "A to K," with each vitamin playing a different role in meeting specific human nutritional needs. Similarly, trust has many essential components that are necessary for it to function optimally for the spiritual, mental, emotional, and social aspects of engaging and positive personal relationships.

Trust, like a multivitamin, has, as essential parts of its core collateral virtues: truthfulness, honesty, fairness, integrity, transparency, faithfulness, sincerity, credibility, reliability, and dependability. For trust to operate optimally in any relationship between God and man, parent and child, and person to person, all the above-mentioned components, which themselves are virtues, must come into play with intentionality and consistency. Trust is betrayed and broken when any one of the above graces become inoperable in interpersonal relationships. It is the responsibility of parents to initiate a trust-building relationship with their children and then teach them that mutual trust is a two-way essential in building loving and caring relationships with others.

What is Trust?

Trust is the nucleus of relationships. It is the mission statement of relationships between God and each person, and that person and other people. Without trust, parents cannot win the confidence of their children and neither can children win the confidence of their parents. In the absence of trust, there will essentially also be an absence of the modeling of any of the virtues of Christ to children. Without the presence of living, active trust, all relationships between a person and God, and that person and other people eventually die. Trust is such an essential virtue for children and adults that it can be justifiably regarded as a "super virtue." Someone has said that, "Most of what we do with and for other people is based upon trust, which is the basis of all business and relationships." No relationship will be long-lived without the presence of mutual trust between the parties.

In the Greek Language, "trust, belief, and faith" share the same root word–*pisteou*. So to trust in something or someone is to also believe in, and have faith in them. As humans we trust a pilot to fly us safely across the ocean. We also trust our doctor that she or he will prescribe the right medication for our healing. We trust the post office to deliver the mail we placed in the mailbox. Similarly we place our trust in people or in God, believing that they will meet our expectations, thus validating our trust in them.

Of the many definitions of trust I have read, three are especially relevant to this discussion on this "super virtue." The first is: "Trust is the firm reliance upon the integrity, ability, or character of a person or thing." The second is: "Trust means being able to predict what other people will do and what situations will occur." The third is: "Trust means making an exchange with someone when you do not have full knowledge about them, their intent and the things they are offering to you" *(The American Heritage Dictionary)*.

There is, however, a fourth aspect of trust that almost defies definition. It is that gut feeling or intuition that is unique to each person, and which gives a person the "go" or "no go" signal to place or withhold their confidence in someone or something. No one can make that call for a person, except those involved in the exchange of trust in a relationship.

The Genesis of Trust

Trust is a self-emergent virtue—it is involuntarily triggered at birth. Unlike many of the other virtues, a child (unknowingly to self or to others) begins to develop a sense of trust from birth. The survival instinct is very strong in living organisms, particularly in humans. So children begin to develop trust as a survival strategy. In their own way, though not cognitively aware, children begin to trust their mother and father to do certain things for them at a certain time. They learn to predict the behavior of the adults around them, and therefore build their trust on the fulfillment of their expectations on a consistent basis.

Infants will jump from an elevated position into the arms of their parent, because they trust their parent will not allow them to fall and get hurt. Trust is a delicate thing. It can be destroyed by one single careless act or made to grow by a single positive act. It is easier to help a child build trust in an atmosphere of honesty, openness, integrity, truthfulness, reliability, than it is to help them build it after it has been broken because of the failure of others to be trustworthy with them. Trust is one of those virtues that become more difficult to build and embrace after it has been repeatedly violated or broken.

The Value of Trust

Trust is the basic building block of all relationships. Without trust, children will not develop positive, engaging relationships with parents, each other, adults, with their spouses later in life, with God, or with anyone for that matter. Trust draws people together. Mistrust separates them and keeps them apart.

When Jesus was on earth, little children would frequently gather around Him to embrace Him and listen to His stories, for they trusted Him. They saw in His compassionate countenance and demeanor that He valued them and desired to be with them. They also saw that His motive was to do them good and not harm. Children are very perceptive; they will often see beyond the actions of a person and discern the attitude that motivates them to act. Although children are born with a sinful nature, they should be trusted and not viewed as having an evil intent in everything they do. The process of learning to trust others and be trusted by others is a lifelong journey. But it is a journey worth pursuing with delicate sensitivity and positive regard for the childlike innocence of little children.

Credibility Quotient (CQ)

Every being, divine or human, young or old, has a credibility quotient (CQ). It is akin to every person having an intelligence quotient (IQ). The credibility quotient (trustworthiness) of a person is determined by several factors: promises made and promises fulfilled. A high CQ involves truthfulness, honesty, fairness, integrity, transparency, faithfulness, sincerity, reliability, and dependability. The indwelling and manifestation of these virtues constitute the CQ of a person. Let me expand on a couple of the factors that they are integrally involved in having a God-approved CQ. God Himself has a CQ of 1:1. That is, the promises He makes, divided by the promises He fulfills is equal to 1. God has never failed to keep His promises to mankind. And He never will! In other words, He has a perfect CQ. That is the enviable standard for all believers.

In raising children, parents and the other adults that are charged with the responsibility of educating them, can and should help them in the trust-building process by faithfully keeping the promises made to them. Children are very sensitive to how adults treat them, and broken promises can destroy their trust, which is the primary building block of their emerging relationships with adults. When adults fail to be reliable and dependable, the trust of children is almost irreparably ruined.

Integrity is another key factor in trust building. When parents and adults do not live lives of integrity—moral purity, transparency, honesty, and truthfulness, they not only damage their children's tender tendrils of trust, but also model behaviors that negatively influence them. Children learn what they live and live what they learn. Unfortunately, vices seem easier to learn and practice than virtues.

Alan K. Simpson, a former U.S. Senator once said, "With integrity, nothing else matters; and without integrity, nothing else matters." Integrity means everything in trust building.

How to Build Trust

Developing a trusting relationship between child and parent is a principal goal of parenting. Trust, like other essential components of a relationship, takes time and much effort to build, but it can be destroyed in a moment. It is incumbent upon parents to take the initiative in being a trustworthy person, then helping their children to build trust in themselves and in others, and ultimately in God. If parents want to teach their children about trust in a relationship, they must teach them what it's like to be able to trust someone and what a trusting relationship looks like. They need to provide a model for their children to see a relationship that is built on trust, showing to them that they have trustworthy parents. This modeling of trust provides a powerful example that children can emulate. It also allows them to engage in a trusting relationship with their parents. This, in turn, provides them with the building blocks upon which relationships with God and others can be built.

When I was growing up, I would often hear stories of parents who would ask their children to tell a lie on their behalf. A common scenario was when someone who the parents do not want to visit with comes to the door of their home. The children would be instructed to tell the visitor that, "My parents are not at home." That simple sentence and act can cause an immediate deconstruction of trust in that parent. When children are being taught to lie, to be dishonest, and to do whatever is necessary to protect their interest, they are led to believe that it is okay to be less than honest and truthful at all times. God hates lying lips (Proverbs 12:22), and lying lips destroy trust and relationships in a hurry. Truthfulness is a pivotal component for building and maintaining trusting relationships.

Trusting Children

Trust is a two-way virtue. When children are trusted, they learn to trust others. Children should be trusted and not have to live under a perpetual cloud of suspicion. Redemptive forces thrive better in an atmosphere of mutual trust and confidence in each other, than in one of suspicion and distrust. Ellen White wisely notes:

> Children and youth are benefited by being trusted. Many, even of the little children, have a high sense of honor; all desire to be treated with confidence and respect, and this is their right. They should not be led to feel that they cannot go out and come in without being watched. Suspicion demoralizes, producing the very evils it seeks to prevent.... Lead the youth to feel that they are trusted, and there are few who will not prove themselves worthy of the trust.[32]

Children will always make mistakes for they are learning daily how to successfully navigate the multiple challenges they face in dealing with building relationships with parents, peers, adults, and ultimately with God. When a child breaks the trust between herself or himself and her or his parents, it becomes the parents' duty to take the initiative and be redemptive in their actions–allowing the child the opportunity to rebuild trust. As children grow and relate to their parents, this parent-initiated redemptive activity will undoubtedly be repeated over and over again. If parents violate trust and break the trust between their child and themselves, they should also take the initiative and apologize to their children, and do whatever it takes to help their child rebuild trust in them. Humility is a signal virtue in trust-building activities.

Trust Mother and Father ... Trust Jesus

The principal goal for helping children to develop and practice the virtue of trust is to lead them to trust Jesus as their friend and Savior. Parents, more than anyone else, represent God to their children. If children can learn to trust mother and father, then they will find it easier to trust their heavenly Father, for their earthly parents will have instilled in them a positive image of their heavenly parents.

Without trust in Jesus, children will not be able to cherish a sense of forgiveness of their sins, or to show confidence in their ability to live triumphantly through God's grace. No trust in God, no saving relationship with Him either! When children learn to trust God, they will also learn to trust in His creative, restorative and redemptive power. They will also trust in the power of His Word to cleanse their sinful lives (Psalm 119:9), the power of His Word to help them resist the Devil (Psalm 119:11), and in the power of His Word to guide their feet into the paths of righteousness (Psalm 119:105). Parents should begin the trust-building work in their children from their infancy so that trust in Jesus may happen at an early age.

HOW TO TEACH TRUST

- Become a person of trust–transparent, reliable, credible, honest, and humble.
- Make no promises to children that you cannot keep. Be honest with them when you answer their questions.
- By precept and example, show children that trust helps to make relationships better.
- Never lie to a child nor ask a child to tell a lie.
- Teach children to, "Speak the truth and speak it ever, cost it what it may."
- Talk about trust with your children regularly, throughout their childhood and teenage years. There is never a time to stop talking about honesty and trust.
- Trust your child to do right. Trust behaves generally like a boomerang–if you give it away, it comes right back to you.

- Practice trust-building activities using age-appropriate language, explaining to your child exactly what you are attempting to do.
- Manifest trust in Jesus and help your child to do likewise.
- Reinforce trustworthy behaviors with appropriate praise and rewards.
- When trust is broken, talk about it and about what it will take to rebuild it.
- **FAMILY ACTIVITY:** Discuss and document more ways in which you can teach the virtue of trust to children

SUMMARY

Trust and truth are twin sisters. Trust is the cornerstone of relationships. Without it, engaging and lasting relationships among humans and between God and humankind cannot be built and sustained. Children are naturally trusting in their nature, and that tender virtue should be carefully nurtured so they will have positive relationship with the people they encounter in life, and most importantly with God their Maker and Savior.

Trust ... no human relationship grows without it! Trust, in both God and in people, leads to obedience and obedience leads to loving and transforming relationships. The ultimate goal of God is that all mankind will be saved. This will not happen because of what any person can and will do. The salvation of humankind will only happen when a person learns to *trust* in what Jesus has done for that person—dying on the cross and forgiving all humankind's sins. Trust in Jesus, therefore, is the pivotal virtue that determines where each created child of God will spend eternity—in heaven with the rightful Daddy.

9
Virtue Review

God has promised that in the last days, He will pour out His Spirit on our sons and daughters (Joel 2:28). This special outpouring of the Spirit will equip our children to not only live sanctified lives, but also to do a special work of helping to prepare and reap the harvest of the earth. There is no doubt that we have arrived in the time of those promised last days in which our Spirit-filled children will be empowered to do a special work for God. What a divine privilege and honor!

If as parents, grandparents, teachers, pastors, counselors, and health care professionals, we succeed in changing the world of a single child, we will have succeeded in changing the whole world. As we nurture and train children for the kingdom of heaven, let us first be the change we want to see in them. Then let us diligently and unceasingly look for the teachable moments in their lives, and impart to them, by precept and example, these seven cardinal virtues of godly living—reverence, obedience, order, meditation, surrender, generosity, and trust. For indeed, the choices that we make for our children today are the choices that *will* make them, and that they will probably make tomorrow.

Even as I write the concluding words of this book, an incredible story is unfolding on the CNN news. It is a true story that actually took place in Argentina. A young mother gave birth to a baby girl in a hospital. The baby was declared to be still born–dead at birth. The baby was quickly taken away by the hospital staff and placed in the hospital's morgue until the parents could make final arrangements for her burial. However, the young mother insisted that she see her baby. After over 10 hours in the ice-cold morgue, the supposedly dead baby received a visit from her grieving parents. When the door of the morgue was opened, the baby moved, and showed other signs of life. She was quickly removed from the morgue and lovingly and warmly cuddled in her mother's arms. This baby girl was born to live!

After many weeks in the hospital, the little girl was finally well enough to go home. She was subsequently released to go home in the arms of one *very thankful* mother. I hope that the story will end something like this, "and they lived happily ever after," on earth and in the eternal kingdom of God! What a way to start life–to be declared DOA–dead on arrival! Someone in that hospital will have some very serious explaining to do and probably a very stressful and haunting law suit to worry about!

If it is true that "all is well that ends well," then this is a classic example of that truth. An intuitive and anxious mother changed the world of a little girl, and she will no doubt change the world also. She has already changed the statistics of babies who were born alive or dead.

Our children were all born dead–alive physically, but spiritually dead because of the spiritual abnormality with which the Devil endowed them. But God does not give up on them at birth and neither does He place them in the morgue of eternal doom. Even before our children were born, God declared that He would fight with those who fight against them and us, and He would save our children (Isaiah 49:25). I am very confident that before long our children will be going home to heaven in the loving arms of their forever Savior and friend. For God's number one goal for our children is that they will be saved and live with Him eternally.

Shouldn't that be the number one goal of parents as well? For it will profit us nothing if we gained all the success that the world offers—money, fame, power, possessions—yet in the end lose our children to the kingdom of the evil one. Indeed, no amount of success in this life will compensate for the loss of one child from the kingdom of God and to the kingdom of the devil.

SUMMARY

As your children grow older they will discover that the best school of all was the School of Virtues where they learned the values of God's kingdom that would make them prosperous and successful in this life and beyond. Kingdom living begins with kingdom virtues. In the words of Sir Henry Newbolt (1862-1938), a British poet, may your children declare that the School of Virtues was their best school:

> It's good to see the school we knew, the land of
> youth and dream.
> To greet again the rule we knew, before we took
> the stream.
> Though long we've missed the sight of her, our
> hearts may not forget,
> We've lost the old delight of her; we'll keep her
> honor yet.

In the words of Paul, I entreat you: " Whatever is true, whatever is noble, whatever is right, whatever is pure, whatever is lovely, whatever is admirable—if anything is excellent and praiseworthy—think on these things" (Philippians 4:8).

The following chart outlines the seven virtues that have been discussed. It also documents some of the requisite, age-appropriate skills that children should display as they grow, learn and understand the value of possessing the seven virtues. As they incorporate them into their lives, they will grow toward faith maturity in "wisdom and stature and in favor with God and man." This sanctifying growth is made possible through the indwelling of the Holy Spirit. It is a steady growth that transforms our precious children into the "image of their Maker" and into becoming godly offspring for the kingdom of heaven. That is true, eternal, untarnishable success that transcends time and eternity!

VIRTUE	SKILLS DEMONSTRATED
Reverence	Respect for God and holy things
	Reverence in the presence of God
	Living in the consciousness of God's constant presence
Obedience	Obedience to parents and other authorities
	Honoring parents
	Obedience to God's commandments
	Self government
Order	Organization in personal life
	Respect for time
	Practicing sequencing
Meditation	Consistent devotional life of prayer and the reading of God's Word daily
	Hiding Scripture in the heart by memorizing it
	Making life's choices based upon guidance from God's Word
Surrender	Experiencing the new birth
	Choosing Christ as the Master of one's life
	Asking God to guide one's pathway in all things great or small
Generosity	Having a heart of compassion and caring
	Sharing with others in need
	Giving back–generosity to God in tithe and offerings

Trust	Being a trustworthy person
	Keeping promises
	Thinking the best of others

Now that the seven virtues as presented in this book have become a part of your child's life, why not work on modeling and teaching seven more virtues—kindness, patience, morality, honesty, forgiveness, compassion, and self-control. And then, yet another seven as your child matures—tolerance, justice, courtesy, loyalty, integrity, humility, and endurance. And still there are myriads of collateral virtues that can be studied, imbibed, and lived. Why not go on a seek-and-find!

And remember always that you may not see the immediate impact of your modeling and teaching, but keep in mind that the body responds consciously or subconsciously to any thought, idea, or motive that the mind embraces. What your children are to be, they are now becoming. When you have done your due diligence in training your children, your next best approach to helping them is to pray without ceasing!

As you thank God for the gift of your children and help them grow into God-honoring, capable, and responsible citizens of His kingdom, may you accept anew, your responsibility as a God-honoring parent, who represents the love, compassion, and purity of God to them. And while you do, consider the words of the poem below:

The Last Word

Parental Success

God has given every parent a special work to do
The most difficult task that humans can undertake;
Children are God's talents to us—to some He gave one
To others two or three and to some even more'
With one eternal and paramount goal in mind
He has given them to us—children of every kind.

We have one chance only to raise them for Him,
To make them into godly offspring, spiritual champions;
And one chance it is, there can be no recall to retrofit
For retrofitting is near impossible with flesh and blood.
So ready, set, go! Give it your best effort!
For soon He'll return and call for a detailed report.

Someday when it really, really matters most
How will you at last measure parental success?
By whose standard will you make up your account?
About His heritage on loan to you for a while;
Have you cared for the children He so lovingly gave?
Did you take the easy road or were you valiantly brave?

Parental success, how is it really measured?
Is it not by the godly offspring that you prayerfully raised?
And by the spiritual champions now serving the Lord?
Is it not by the children who have hid His Word?
In their hearts so that against Him they might not sin;
But against the Devil every battle was a special win.

Is it not by children who know that there's a difference
Between the holy and the common?

By children who increased in wisdom and stature,
And in favor with God and man;
Is it not by children who are generous and kind?
Who know how to help others, even the blind?

Is it not by children who can say 'no' to drugs?
And live a pure life and flee sexual immorality;
By children who take seriously their personal devotion
And practice honesty, nobility, and chastity;
By children, who from the days of their youth,
Honored their Creator and His word of truth?

Is it not by children who are taught to be clean and orderly?
Who know how to clean up after themselves?
Who courteously say, "yes ma'am, yes sir,"
And never forgetting "please" and "thank you" to say?
Children who honor their mother and their father
And who treat each person they meet as a brother.

How do you measure parental success?
It is *not* by the size of your house, or of your multiple cars,
And neither is it by the size and number of flat screens,
Or of your gadgets, so modern and top of the line;
The flights and cruises you take will certainly not count
When your Master calls on you to give an account.

How do you measure parental success?
It certainly is *not* by your child's accomplishments
Their diplomas, and medals and trophies of gold,
If Christ they did not know and love and serve;
Only the things that have eternal value will really matter
For everything else is worth nothing in the hereafter.

How do you measure parental success?
How will you fare when He comes and inquires?
About the "little flock" that He left in your care?
Will you with joy return to Him His heritage?
Saying, "Lord, I did my best though it was taxing,"
To raise them as spiritual champions and godly offspring!

L. Roo McKenzie, 2010

Endnotes

1 *Newsweek*, May 31, 2004
2 books.google.com/books?id=wks5AQAAMAAJ&pg=PA15&lpg=PA15
3 Bennett, William J. The Book of Virtues, p.11; Simon and Shuster; New York 1993
4 Bennett, William J; The Book of Virtues, p. 17, Simon and Shuster, New York, 1993
5 Singer-Freeman, Karen E. Concrete operational Period, Encyclopedia of Human Development, Vol. 1, Thousand Oaks, CA, 2006
6 Sally Shaywitz, Educational Leadership, Vol. 60, April 2003
7 White, Ellen. G; Child Guidance, Nashville, Tennessee: Southern Publishing Association, 1904, p. 193
8 Michaelson, Johanna, Like Lambs to the Slaughter, Harvest House Publishers, 1992, p. 129
9 Luke 2: 52
10 White, Ellen G. Education, Mountain View, California, Pacific Press Publishing Association, 1903 p. 241
11 Farley, William P; Gospel-Powered Parenting, page 31, P&R Publishing, New Jersey, 2009
12 White, Ellen G. Education, Mountain View, California, Pacific Press Publishing Association, 1903 p. 241
13 Luke 2:52
14 http://www.hymntime.com/tch/htm/g/e/n/gentleje.htm
15 Bloom, Alan; The Closing of the American Mind, Simon and Shuster, New York, p. 57
16 Twenge, Jean M. Generation Me, The Free press, New York, 2006. P. 30
17 White, Ellen G. Education, Mountain View, California, Pacific Press Publishing Association, **1903, p.**
18 White, Ellen G. Testimonies to The Church, Pacific Press Publishing Association, **1904,** Mountain View, California, Vol.4 p. 202

19 White, Ellen G. Patriarchs and Prophets, Pacific Press Publishing Association, Mountain View, California, p.579

20 Evans, Tony; The Promise, Moody Press, Chicago, 1996, p.266

21 Dobson, James. Children At Risk, WORD Publishing Group, Dallas, 1992, p. 5

22 Farley, William P; Gospel-Powered Parenting, P&R Publishing, New Jersey, 2009, p. 24

23 Luke 2: 52

24 M'Chenye, Robert M. (1813-18430) Sermon # 11,

25 Farley, William P; Gospel-Powered Parenting, P&R Publishing, New Jersey, 2009, p. 49

26 AWNSA Journal, Waldorf Education; The Essential Phases of Child Development, 2015

27 White, Ellen. G, Child Guidance Nashville, Tennessee: Southern Publishing Association, 1954, p. 256

28 Luke 2: 52

29 Barna, George; Transforming Children into Spiritual Champions, Regal Books, California, 1996, p. 34

30 Twenge, Jean M. Generation Me, The Free Press, New York, 2006, p. 1

31 Twenge, Jean M. Generation Me, The Free Press, New York, 2006. P. 4

32 White, Ellen G. Education, Mountain View, California, Pacific Press Publishing Association, 1903, p. 289

Printed in the United States
By Bookmasters